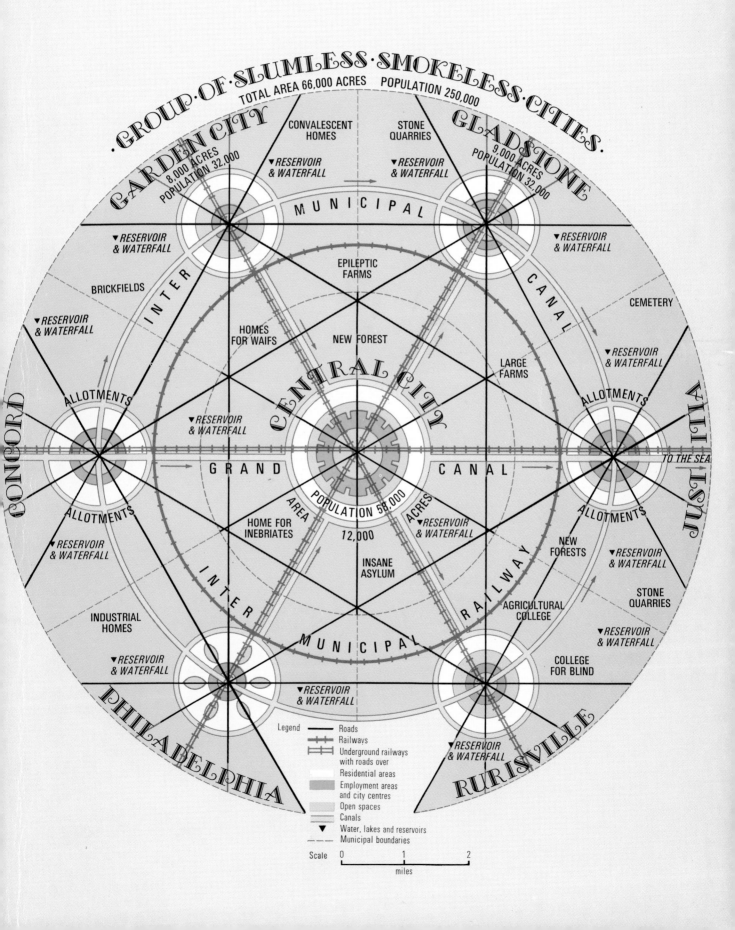

GROUP·OF·SLUMLESS·SMOKELESS·CITIES.

TOTAL AREA 66,000 ACRES   POPULATION 250,000

GARDEN CITY
8,000 ACRES
POPULATION 32,000

GLADSTONE
9,000 ACRES
POPULATION 32,000

CONVALESCENT HOMES

STONE QUARRIES

▼ RESERVOIR & WATERFALL

▼ RESERVOIR & WATERFALL

MUNICIPAL

▼ RESERVOIR & WATERFALL

▼ RESERVOIR & WATERFALL

INTER

CANAL

EPILEPTIC FARMS

BRICKFIELDS

CEMETERY

▼ RESERVOIR & WATERFALL

HOMES FOR WAIFS

NEW FOREST

▼ RESERVOIR & WATERFALL

CENTRAL CITY

LARGE FARMS

ALLOTMENTS

ALLOTMENTS

CONCORD

JUSTITIA

▼ RESERVOIR & WATERFALL

GRAND   CANAL

TO THE SEA

ALLOTMENTS

POPULATION 58,000

ALLOTMENTS

AREA   ACRES

NEW FORESTS

HOME FOR INEBRIATES

12,000

▼ RESERVOIR & WATERFALL

▼ RESERVOIR & WATERFALL

▼ RESERVOIR & WATERFALL

INSANE ASYLUM

INTER

RAILWAY

STONE QUARRIES

INDUSTRIAL HOMES

AGRICULTURAL COLLEGE

▼ RESERVOIR & WATERFALL

MUNICIPAL

COLLEGE FOR BLIND

▼ RESERVOIR & WATERFALL

▼ RESERVOIR & WATERFALL

PHILADELPHIA

RURISVILLE

▼ RESERVOIR & WATERFALL

Legend
— Roads
+—+ Railways
▭ Underground railways with roads over
☐ Residential areas
▨ Employment areas and city centres
▨ Open spaces
— Canals
▼ Water, lakes and reservoirs
- - - Municipal boundaries

Scale 0   1   2
                miles

The Open University

80p

Social Sciences : a second level course Urban development Unit 26

The new town idea

Prepared for the Course Team
by Ray Thomas and Peter Cresswell

The Open University Press

Front Cover: Howard's proposal for a system of smokeless cities.
(Note: part of this diagram is reproduced as Figure 4)
Source: Ebenezer Howard, *Tomorrow: a Peaceful Path to Real Reform*, Sonnenschein, 1898

Back Cover: Milton Keynes – the strategic plan. Note that the plan has been drawn to
the same scale as that for Howard's diagram on the front cover
Source: Milton Keynes Development Corporation. *The Plan for Milton Keynes, Volume 1*

The Open University Press
Walton Hall Milton Keynes

First published 1973

Designed by the Media Development Group of the Open University.

Printed in Great Britain by
COES THE PRINTERS LIMITED
RUSTINGTON SUSSEX

1 SBN 0 335   01751 7

This text forms part of the correspondence element of an Open University Second Level
Course. The complete list of units in the course is given at the end of this text.

For general availability of supporting material referred to in this text, please write to the
Director of Marketing, The Open University, Walton Hall, Milton Keynes, MK7 6AA.

Further information on Open University courses may be obtained from the Admissions
Office, The Open University, P.O. Box 48, Milton Keynes, MK7 6AA.

The new town idea

1 Aims and objectives
Aims

The aim of this unit is to give an account of the history of the new town idea and to discuss the British experience of new towns. The concentration on the British experience is appropriate because both the new town idea and its application are more developed in the UK than in any other country of the western world.

But new towns are not an easy subject for study by social scientists. In Britain as in some other countries there is a polarization of views on the subject. On the one hand there is what is often described as a new towns movement led in Britain by the Town and Country Planning Association and tacitly supported by a significant proportion of the town planning profession. On the other hand there are many who believe that there is more ideology than ideas in the new towns. There are many who are against the concentration of powers in the planning process particularly in the context of the development of new towns, and who would like to see a greater dispersion of decision making power. Many of these would also object to the level of public expenditure involved. A further group claim that the new towns have failed to achieve their social goals (which are discussed in Section 5) and that settlements placed arbitrarily and lacking any long history of growth and development are bound to suffer from a lack of 'character' and an architectural sameness.

This polarization of views is mirrored in studies made of urban development. A large proportion of studies of new towns are made by enthusiastic practitioners whose perceptions may be clouded by their enthusiasm. There are no studies of substance which systematically compare new towns with other forms of urban development. Most students of urban development focus their interests on some aspects of the city itself and ignore what is happening at the fringe. Apart from some brief discussion in Blumenfeld, for example, there is scarcely a mention of new towns in any of the set books for the course.

This unit has been written by two authors who are from different disciplines (economics and sociology) and who have different perspectives on planning and the new towns. We have aimed in this unit to provide the necessary factual basis for a discussion of the new town idea and also a conspectus of views about new towns. Sections 2, 3 and 8 of this unit were written by Ray Thomas. Sections 4 and 5 were written jointly, and Sections 6 and 7 were written by Peter Cresswell. You may well detect a number of divergencies of view in this unit. This is because the aim is to provide an account which will enable you to criticize, appraise and recognize the assumptions underlying the arguments which are put forward both by proponents and opponents of the new town idea.

You should note that this unit concentrates on new towns which are intended as a means of accommodating metropolitan growth. Not all new towns are designed to fulfil this purpose. The new town idea has also been used as an instrument for regional development – as in the case of Glenrothes in Scotland. New towns have been built in order to provide centres of urban facilities for rural areas (Newtown in Wales) or for a scattered collection of mining villages (Peterlee in County Durham). New towns have been developed to accommodate the growth of particular industries (such as Corby in Northamptonshire and Durgapur in India, both of which serve steelworks). In a number of countries 'new towns' have been promoted to constitute a new capital city (Washington, DC and Canberra are the classic examples; Brasilia, Islamabad in Pakistan, and Chandigarh the capital of the Punjab are more recent examples). But this unit concentrates upon an analysis of the idea of new towns and its relationship to attempts to solve the growth problems of major cities.

After studying this unit you should be able to:

1 Outline the origin and main features of the new town idea.
2 List and describe the characteristics which distinguish what are usually called new towns from those of other forms of metropolitan growth.
3 Explain the following terms:
   development corporation
   expanded town
   'self-contained'
   'balanced'
   job ratio
   index of commuting independence
4 Discuss the functions of words such as 'community' in the process of a new town development.
5 Explain with examples, how the aims of the new town development corporation are achieved through indirect controls and how individuals and individual organizations are able to achieve their relevant goals through a process of strategic interaction.
6 Evaluate the success of Britain's satellite new towns.

What you have to do

You will be able to achieve objectives 1, 3, 4 and 5 on the basis of study of this unit alone. To help achieve objective 2 you should look again at Unit 24, 'Suburban and exurban growth', because new towns are usually regarded as an alternative to suburban growth.

Objective 6 has been deliberately formulated in an open ended way. The success or otherwise of the new towns can be assessed on many different criteria. They can be assessed, for example, in relation to whether or not they have achieved their stated aims, upon whether or not they meet the needs of their inhabitants, on their contribution to a solution of the problems of their parent city, or on purely financial grounds. The success or otherwise of the new towns on some of these criteria can be assessed on the basis of the contents of this unit. But in order fully to achieve this objective you should relate the contents of this unit to what you have learnt from other parts of the course – in particular Unit 23 which discusses some of the metropolitan problems new towns were intended to help solve, and Unit 24 which describes the process of suburban growth – the major 'natural' growth process which can be compared with and contrasted to new town development.

2 Ebenezer Howard and the new town movement

The idea of new towns was a response to the industrialization and rapid urbanization of the nineteenth century. In terms of rates of growth, towns and cities grew in the nineteenth century at rates comparable with those of new towns in the twentieth century. But the conditions of growth were very different. According to all shades of political opinion – from revolutionaries like Frederick Engels, social reformers like Edwin Chadwick and public officials like John Simon – cities were places of overcrowding, poverty, crime, disease, insanitary conditions and potential revolution (see, for example, Ashworth 1954 Chapter III).

As far as physical health is concerned these conditions led to what seem to be the first estimates of life expectancy. In the 1840s William Farr the Registrar General estimated that the average expectancy of life in England and Wales was 41 years. In London it was 37, in Liverpool 26 and in Manchester 24. In the 1870s Farr made what must be one of the first attempts at a cost/benefit analysis. He estimated that by bringing up England as a whole to the standard of healthy districts (where the average mean life time was 49 years) the economic value of the population would be increased by £1,050 millions (Ashworth 1954 pp 59–60).

Table 1 Population of the principal cities of Britain 1801–1901

City	Population (thousands)		
	1801	1851	1901
Greater London	1,117	2,685	6,586
Birmingham	71	233	761
Bradford	13	104	280
Bristol	61	137	339
Edinburgh (incl. Leith)	83	202	395
Glasgow	77	375	918
Leeds	53	172	429
Liverpool	82	395	704
Manchester	75	339	645
Sheffield	46	135	409
Rest of Great Britain	9,008	16,102	25,625
Total Great Britain	**10,686**	**20,879**	**37,091**

Notes: Includes all cities with a population of more than 250,000 in 1901.
Some of the figures may understate the population of the cities in 1801 and 1851 in the sense that they do not cover the same area as 1901. As cities have expanded the administrative boundary has often been extended. Only in the case of Greater London are data available for the same area for the whole period.

Source: Mitchell, B.R. and Deane, Phyllis (1962) *Abstract of British Historical Statistics,* Cambridge University Press

Many reformers at that time saw a solution to these urbanization problems in terms of new settlements. Robert Owen (1771–1858) took over a cotton mill and industrial village at New Lanark in Scotland in 1799 and devoted all the surplus profits of the enterprise to the provision of social services. He enlarged houses to relieve overcrowding, opened a co-operative shop, abolished child labour, set up a school and built up an Institute for the Formation of Character, which was used for children during the day and by adults in the evening. Owen's writings included *Villages of Unity and Mutual Co-operation* which

Figure 1 New Lanark Source: Mansell Collection

proposed model towns of 800–1,200 inhabitants. Perhaps because he held anti-religious views Owen's ideas were not adopted in Britain though three 'ideal villages' were founded in America (Burke 1971 pp 135–6).

Figure 2 **New Victoria** Source: J. S. Buckingham, *National Evils and Practical Remedies* (1849)

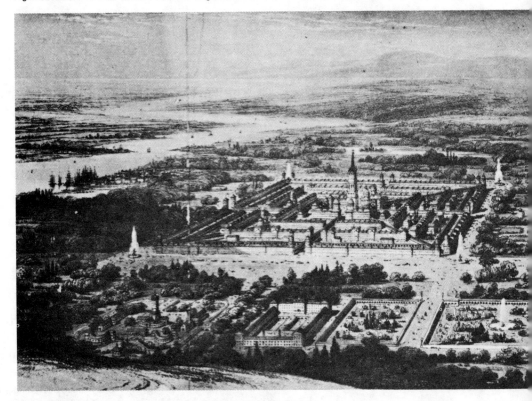

James Silk Buckingham published in 1849 an elaborate proposal for a New Town called Victoria under the title *National Evils and Practical Remedies*. His model town would be built and managed by a joint stock company. The town itself would be a mile square with not more than 10,000 inhabitants but it would be surrounded by 10,000 acres of farmland. There would be free education, medical treatment, libraries and public baths. There would be a private water closet for each dwelling with rents ranging from £10 to £300 per annum. The innermost square of the town would accommodate 'members of the government and the more opulent capitalists' together with the main public buildings. The outermost square would house the 'lowest orders'.

Titus Salt established a factory employing 3,000 people on a site four miles north of Bradford in the 1850s. He provided housing, water supply and drainage, a chapel and a church, a club, a library and many other public buildings. This new town of Saltaire still retains a separate visual identity and is locally known as 'The Village' (Burke 1971 p 143).

In 1875 Sir Benjamin Ward Richardson proposed to the Social Science Research Council a comprehensively planned city of 100,000 population, *Hygea: The City of Health*. Hygea was conceived of as being large enough to contain a cross section of the national population and a wide range of employment opportunities. Most important 'the perfection of sanitary results will be approached if not realised in the co-existence of the lowest possible general mortality rate with the highest possible individual longevity' (Richardson 1876 p 10).

Towards the end of the nineteenth century W. H. Lever built the model town of Port Sunlight in Cheshire to house the workers of his soap factory. George

Cadbury built Bournville village to house the workers of his chocolate factory. Both of these developments were at relatively low densities (originally 5–8 houses per acre) and were successful in financial terms.

Parallel to this rejection of the existing pattern of urban growth came a romantic idealization of country life as opposed to life in the city. In addition to being seen as crowded, congested, polluted and noisy, cities were seen as too complex and too large to be comprehended by a simple and unitary intellectual act. This rejection of the city led to a concentration in literature, particularly in poetry, on the rural scene (Peterson 1969).

Urbanization problems in the nineteenth century and the new town solution were not confined to Britain. George H. Pullman relocated his industrial plant in 1867 to Pullman City near Chicago where houses had running water and sewage disposal and public buildings including a theatre with 1,000 seats. Etienne Cabet organized new settlements in Texas and Iowa. Krupp built a number of workers' settlements in Germany in the late nineteenth century – Schederdorf, Atendorf, Alfredshof and Margarenthof. An industrialist named Van Marken, built Agneta Park round a lake in Holland in the 1880s. Charles Fourier inspired the building of Guise designed by the industrialist Jean Baptiste Godin. A Spaniard Arturo Soria y Mata pioneered the idea of a new linear city based on railway transport in 1882. Tony Garnier at the turn of the century proposed a detailed design of a *cite industrielle* of 35,000 inhabitants (Choay 1972).

None of these experiments or utopias however seems to have had a major lasting influence on urban development. One reason for this is perhaps that they concentrated too much on single aspects of new town development. New towns based on a single industry were vulnerable to trade fluctuations. Utopias inspired mainly by ideas for sanitary reform or architecture were unlikely to appeal to industrialists or public servants conscious of their financial responsibilities. According to Ashworth the major ideological obstacle to any kind of measure for urban improvement was the zeal for economy in public administration. He quotes a late nineteenth century pamphlet called *The Face of the Poor or the Crowding of London's Labourers* as saying: 'It seems but idle mockery to talk about pure air and sound lungs. But try to think out a plan and you are met with the hard, impenetrable and unclimbable wall called, WILL IT PAY?' (Quoted in Ashworth 1954 p 67.)

This point was amply discussed by Ebenezer Howard's book *Tomorrow: A Peaceful Path to Real Reform* first published in 1898. Howard, a non-conformist part time inventor and clerk, gathered together the various arguments and proposed that planned dispersal should be effected through the creation of garden cities. The second revised issue of his book published in 1902 was in fact entitled *Garden Cities of Tomorrow*.

Garden Cities of Tomorrow is not a book about architecture, sanitary reform or utopias. These elements of the argument for new towns were, in effect, taken for granted. Howard's book is mainly about urban economics, estate management, and theories of urban growth. Howard, like Henry George, diagnosed the high level of urban rents as the underlying cause of the cities' problems, but he advocated a quite different type of solution:

... Mr Henry George, in his well-known work, *Progress and Poverty*, urges with much eloquence, if not with complete accuracy of reasoning, that our land laws are responsible for all the economic evils of society, and that as our landlords are little better than pirates and robbers, the sooner the State forcibly appropriates their rents the better, for when this is accomplished the problem of poverty will, he suggests, be entirely solved. But is not this attempt to throw the whole blame of and punishment for the present deplorable condition of society on to a single class of men a very great mistake? In what way are landlords as a class less honest than the average citizen? Give the average citizen the opportunity of becoming a landlord and of appropriating the land values created by his tenants, and he will embrace it tomorrow. If then, the average man is a potential landlord, to attack landlords as individuals is very like a nation drawing up an indictment against itself, and then making a scape-goat of a particular class.

But to endeavour to change our land system is a very different matter from attacking those individuals who represent it. But how is this change to be effected? I reply: By the force of example, that is, by setting up a better system . . . (Howard 1965 edition p 136)

Figure 3 Howard's three magnets Source: Howard (1965 edition)

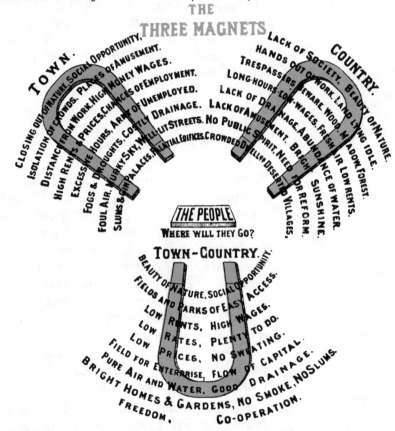

Howard suggested that instead of thinking in terms of a polarization of town and country there should be a merger between the two, to create a 'town-country' element which possessed the advantages of both elements and the disadvantages of neither. His arguments are summarized in the diagram representing three magnets which is reproduced as Figure 3.

The major features emphasized in Howard's proposals were:
1 The town would be built on agricultural land acquired at a low cost.
2 Ownership of the estate would be held in trust by 'gentlemen of undoubted probity and honour'. The money would be raised by mortgage debentures bearing interest at not more than four per cent. All ground rents for property in the town would be paid to the trustees who after interest had been paid would hand over the balance to the council of the town.
3 The town itself would have a population of 30,000. It would have a good variety of employment and a full range of public facilities and buildings.

4 The town estate would have associated agricultural activities – including large farms, smallholdings, allotments, cow pastures – which would utilize the refuse of the town, and which would have a population of about 2,000.

5 The process of growth would be by establishing *another* new town near to the original new town and directly connected by road and rail. As you can see from Figure 4 Howard envisaged that a parent city would grow through the construction of a succession of new towns forming a cluster of centres surrounded by country. You will note that Figure 4 reproduces part of the diagram given on the cover of the unit which illustrates a further development of this growth principle.

Figure 4 Howard's correct principles of city growth Source: Howard (1965 edition)

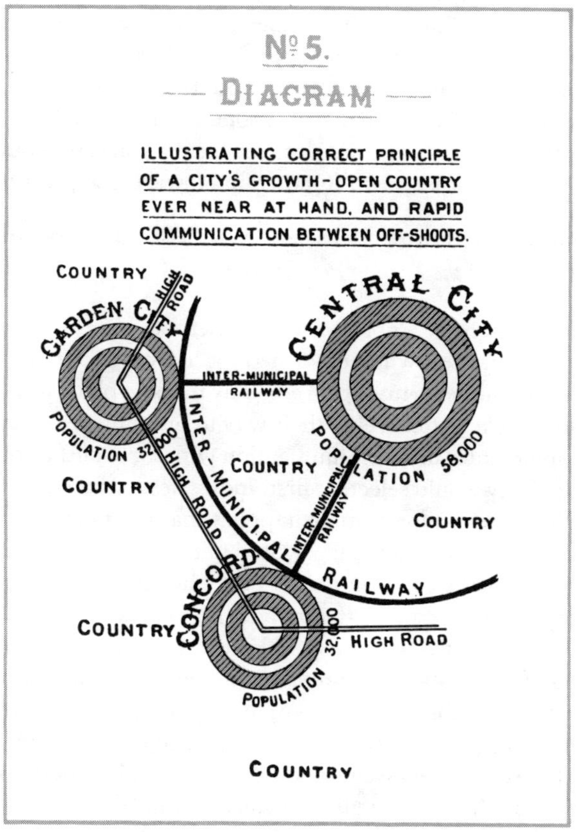

Howard himself claimed that his scheme was a combination of three sets of ideas which had not previously been brought together. These three sets of ideas were:

1 Proposals for organizing the migration of population advocated by Edward Gibbon Wakefield and the economist Alfred Marshall.

2 A system of land tenure proposed by Thomas Spence and the social philosopher Herbert Spencer.

3 The model city of James Silk Buckingham.

Edward Gibbon Wakefield (1796–1862) is described in the *Dictionary of National Biography* as a colonial statesman. At one period of his life he was an advisor to the Governor General of British colonies in North America where he played a part in writing a report which advocated unity of the North American provinces and the granting of full control of their internal affairs. He founded the New Zealand Association which was concerned with questions of annexation and colonization of those islands. Some of Wakefield's relevant ideas were expressed in a pamphlet entitled *A letter from Sydney* in 1829 where he diagnosed as the cause of Australia's economic problems of that time the fact that land could be acquired so easily that no one except convicts was willing to remain as dependents and as a result there was an acute shortage of labourers. Wakefield proposed that the process of converting labourers to landed proprietors should be hindered by abolishing free grants of land and substituting a requirement that payment should be made on the basis of a fixed sum per acre.

The ideas in Wakefield's writings which Howard emphasized were included in *A View of the Art of Colonization* published in 1849. Wakefield advocated that colonies should be based on scientific principles:

... We send out colonies of the limbs, without the belly and the head, of needy persons, many of them mere paupers, or even criminals; colonies made up of *a single class of persons* in the community, and that the most helpless and the most unfit to perpetuate our national character, and to become the fathers of a race whose habits of thinking and feeling shall correspond to those which, in the meantime, we are cherishing at home. The ancients, on the contrary, sent out *a representation of the parent State-colonists from all ranks*. (Quoted in Howard 1965 edition p 119)

Howard related these ideas to those of Alfred Marshall published in an article *The Housing of the London Poor* in 1884:

... There might be a great variety of method, but the general plan would probably be for a committee, whether formed specially for the purpose or not, to interest themselves in the formation of a colony in some place well beyond the range of London smoke. After seeing their way to building or buying suitable cottages there, they would enter into communication with some of the employers of low-waged labour. They would select, at first, industries that used very little fixed capital; and, as we have seen, it fortunately happens that most of the industries which it is important to move are of this kind. They would find an employer – and there must be many such – who really cares for the misery of his employees. Acting with him and by his advice, they would make themselves the friends of people employed or fit to be employed in his trade; they would show them the advantages of moving, and help them to move, both the counsel and money. They would organize the sending of work backwards and forwards, the employer perhaps opening an agency on the colony. But after being once started it ought to be self-supporting, for the cost of carriage, even if the employees went in sometimes to get instructions, would be less than the saving made in rent – at all events, if allowance be made for the value of the garden produce. And more than as much gain would probably be saved by removing the temptation to drink which is caused by the sadness of London. They would meet with much passive resistance at first. The unknown has terrors to all, but especially to those who have lost their natural spring. Those who have lived always in the obscurity of a London court might shrink away from the free light; poor as are their acquaintanceships at home, they might fear to go where they knew no one. But, with gentle insistence, the committee would urge their way, trying to get those who knew one another to move together, by warm, patient sympathy, taking off the chill of the first change. It is only the first step that costs; every succeeding step would be easier. The work of several firms, not always in the same business, might, in some cases, be sent together. Gradually a prosperous industrial district would grow up, and then, more self-interest would induce employers to bring down their main workshops, and even to start factories in the colony. Ultimately all would gain, but most the landlowners and the railroads connected with the colony. (Quoted in Howard 1965 edition pp 121–2)

You will remember that this analogy between colonization and urban migratory movements was also drawn in Unit 24 on the migratory movement to suburbs.

Thomas Spence (1750–1814) was a bookseller and advocate of the municipalization of land. In *The Real Rights of Man* published in 1775 he proposed that the inhabitants of each parish should form a corporation which would own all of the land of the parish. This idea was taken up by Herbert Spencer in his book *Social Statics, or the Conditions Essential to Human Happiness specified, and the first of them developed* (1851). The essential condition was that 'every man has the freedom to do what he wants provided that he infringes not the equal freedom of any other man'. Spencer in discussing land ownership wrote:

... But to what does this doctrine that men are equally entitled to the use of the earth, lead? Must we return to the times of unenclosed wilds, and subsist on roots, berries, and game? Or are we to be left to the management of Messrs Fourier, Owen, Louis Blanc & Co? Neither. Such a doctrine is consistent with the highest civilization, may be carried out without involving a community of goods, and need cause no very serious revolution in existing arrangements. The change required would be simply a change of landlords. Separate ownership would merge in the joint-stock ownership of the public. Instead of being in the possession of individuals, the country would be held by the great corporate body – society. Instead of leasing his acres from an isolated proprietor, the farmer would lease them from the nation. Instead of paying his rent to the agent of Sir John and His Grace, he would pay it to an agent or deputy agent of the community. Stewards would be public officials instead of private ones, and tenancy the only land tenure. A state of things so ordered would be in perfect harmony with the moral law. Under it all men would be equally landlords; all men would be alike free to become tenants. A, B, C and the rest might compete for a vacant farm as now, and one of them might take that farm without in any way violating the principles of pure equity. All would be equally free to bid; all would be equally free to refrain. And when the farm had been let to A, B, or C, all parties would have done that which they willed, the one in choosing to pay a given sum to his fellow men for the use of certain lands – the others in refusing to pay the sum. Clearly, therefore, on such a system the earth might be enclosed, occupied, and cultivated in entire subordination to the law of equal freedom. (*Social Statics*, Chap. IX, sec. 8 quoted in Howard 1965 pp 123–4)

Spencer later withdrew the proposal partly, according to Howard, because he realized that he was in effect advocating the nationalization of land, but also because he could not see a way in which land could be acquired which would both be equitable to existing owners and remunerative to the community.

Howard believed he had the answer to both of Spencer's difficulties. First, the land would not be nationalized but municipalized, or more precisely, held in trust on behalf of the municipality. Second, the acquisition problem would be solved by buying land at agricultural prices and then converting it to urban uses in accordance with the migratory movements advocated by Wakefield and Marshall.

The third set of ideas which Howard claimed contributed to his scheme were those of James Silk Buckingham. Howard rejected the monopolist aspects of Buckingham's model city but wholeheartedly accepted most of its other features. In particular, Howard commended the advantages to be derived from combining an agricultural and industrial employment, quoting a passage from Buckingham's book *National Evils and Practical Remedies*:

... Wherever practicable, the labours of agriculture and manufacture to be so mingled and the variety of fabrics and materials to be wrought upon also so assorted as to make short periods of labour on each alternately with others produce that satisfaction and freedom from tedium and weariness which an unbroken round of monotonous occupation so frequently occasions, and because also variety of employment develops the mental as well as physical faculties much more perfectly than any single occupation. (Quoted in Howard 1965 edition p 126)

Howard's ideas have had a lasting influence. In 1901 he helped establish the Garden City Association which has remained as an active voluntary association advocating metropolitan decentralization and new town development ever since. It is now called the Town and Country Planning Association. In 1903 the First Garden City Ltd Company was formed with a share capital of £300,000 to develop a new town at Letchworth in Hertfordshire. In 1920 the Welwyn Garden City Ltd Company was formed to build a second new town in Hertfordshire. In 1935 the government appointed a departmental committee (the Marley Committee) to:

... examine the experience already gained in regard to the establishment of garden cities ... and satellite towns and to make recommendations as to the steps, if any, which should be taken by the government to extend the provision of such garden cities and satellite towns. (Ministry of Health 1935)

The conclusions and recommendations of the Marley Committee included:

... we advocate the fullest adoption of the type of development usually associated with the idea of the Garden City.
... the dangers and evils, economic and social, which follow from haphazard, scattered and ribbon development can hardly be exaggerated.
... the present tendency to demand for general adoption higher buildings and greater density of occupation in central areas is based upon existing concentrations and the absence of planning in the past, accentuated by the disordered and badly planned suburban development which has taken place in recent years.
... when a town reaches a certain size, which may vary within wide limits, continuous growth round the fringe may create evils that outweigh any advantages; at this stage in its growth any further outward development should take the form of complete planned units each having due provision for industry, residence, social services and recreation. (Ministry of Health 1935 pp 25–6)

You will note that, while the new town idea was being accepted wholeheartedly, a quite new argument had entered the debate. New towns were being advocated as an alternative to the semi-detached suburbia of the interwar period as well as an alternative to the city itself.

In 1940 the Royal Commission on the Distribution of Industrial Population produced its report (The Barlow Report) which gave moderate support to the new town idea. Abercrombie's Greater London Plan of 1944 proposed a constraining Green Belt around London and the overspill of employment and population to ten new towns 20–30 miles from central London. Abercrombie and Matthew's Clyde Regional Plan of 1946 proposed three new towns for Glasgow.

In the same year of 1946 the new Labour government appointed a committee under Lord Reith with the directive:

... to consider the general questions of the establishment, development, organisation and administration that will arise in the promotion of New Towns in furtherance of a policy of planned decentralisation from congested urban areas; and in accordance therewith to suggest guiding principles on which such Towns should be established and developed as self-contained and balanced communities for work and living. (Ministry of Town and Country Planning 1946)

Within months of the first report of this committee the New Towns Act was passed by Parliament.

3 Towards a definition of satellite new towns

There is nowadays no sharp and clear distinction between what are usually called new towns and other forms of metropolitan growth. Many of Britain's new towns are regarded as archetypal because they possess or are intended to possess a combination of features which can be listed under five heads:

1 There is a rapid population growth from a relatively small base.
2 The town is comprehensively planned by a development agency.
3 The town is spatially separate from the parent city and is built on land which has been acquired at a lower cost than that of land at the periphery of the built up area of the city.
4 A large proportion of property in the town remains in the ownership of a non-profit making public body.
5 To summarize a number of features in a single phrase, the towns were intended to be, in accordance with the terms of reference of the Reith Committee, 'self-contained and balanced communities for work and living'.

Many of these features are shared by new towns in other countries but, except perhaps in the communist countries, there are no other developments which can claim to possess all of these features. Rapid population growth from a small base on the scale of the British new towns, for example, occurs in many countries (as you will recall from your study of Unit 24). Some of these developments can claim to be comprehensively planned, some are built on land acquired at a low cost which is situated at some distance from the parent city, but only a minority could be said to be balanced with regard to level of employment relative to population or even relatively balanced with regard to the structure of employment, and none yet built appear to have made as serious an attempt to become socially balanced as the British new towns.

The aim and extent of achievement of social balance and self-containment is the subject matter of Section 5 of this unit. The present purpose is to discuss some of the other features and their relationship to one aspect of the goal of social balance – that is the question of accommodating members of low income groups. The extent to which migrants to new towns include a substantial proportion of members of low income groups depends upon the cost of housing in the new town. This section concentrates therefore on the cost of land and on the other factors which determine the level of rents charged by new town developers.

As you know from Unit 14 land prices decline steeply with increasing distance from the centre of major cities. This decline continues to well beyond the built up area of the city until land prices flatten out at a level corresponding to the use of the land for some kind of agricultural or forestry use. Thus any organization concerned with urban development faces a strategic choice with regard to the location of a development. The development agency, whether a profit seeking firm or a public body of some kind, can choose between a relatively costly site close to the existing built up area or a relatively cheap site at some distance from the city.

A number of factors influence this choice besides the cost of land. One particularly important set of factors is the availability of services such as roads, sewerage, water supply, primary schools, shops, etc. For a site close to the existing built up area the developer may have to meet only a low proportion, if any, of the cost of providing these facilities. There may be only the minimal costs of connection to existing services like sewerage and it may be possible for the new development to depend entirely upon existing schools and shops to meet the needs of its future residents. But for a greenfields site some distance from the city many of these services may have to be paid for by the developer.

If he cannot or does not provide facilities such as paved roads, schools and shops then the lack of these services will detract from the market value of the houses he builds. Where the developer is a small private firm – to take an extreme but typical example – there may effectively be little choice. The small private firm can only take on a handful of houses and is unlikely to have the financial resources which would enable it to provide more than the minimum in the way of ancillary services. These factors limit the choice of the small development agency to small infill sites within or at the edge of the existing built up area. The larger the development agency, the larger in general is the intended scale of development, the larger the financial resources available, and the greater the degree of choice which can be exercised.

One of the considerations which is likely to favour selection by a large agency of a more distant site is the difficulty of land assembly. For land close to the existing built up area it is likely that ownership has already become fragmented by pre-suburban developments. This may make it difficult to acquire a large enough site without having to buy some plots of land which have already passed into some form of urban development – which increases the cost. Fragmentation of ownership also makes the process of acquisition difficult or costly. If the market is alerted to the intended scale of development, land prices will rise. The developer might find that he has to pay much more in terms of cost per unit of land area for those parts of the site he acquires later than those he acquired earlier. A more distant site is often a better prospect because fewer land owners may be involved, and in the extreme case it may be possible for the developer to purchase the whole of the area required for development from a single owner.

Letchworth and Welwyn Garden City (in its growth before official designation as a new town in 1947) as well as many developments in the United States conform to this pattern. Letchworth, for example, is thirty-five miles from central London. The First Garden City Ltd, which was the company formed specifically to promote Ebenezer Howard's ideas, purchased 3,822 acres of land at Letchworth from fifteen different owners at a total cost of £160,000 – or an average of £42 per acre (Purdom 1949 p 54). Welwyn Garden City Ltd originally bought 2,378 acres in the 1920s for a total cost of £106,000 or an average cost of £44 per acre (Purdom 1949 p 188).

In the United States there is at least one company which specializes in large developments at a fair distance from the parent city. Levitt and Sons, a construction company, has so far built three Levittowns. One is on Long Island thirty-five miles from the centre of New York, one is in Bucks County, Pennsylvania about twenty-five miles from the centre of Philadelphia, and one is about seven miles from Trenton in New Jersey. All of these developments are dormitory suburban in character without any substantial volume of employment. But with populations in the range of 60–70,000 they are just about the same size as the typical British new town.

Many other developments in the United States are on this scale – or even larger. In general the developing agency either purchased the land from a single owner or the developing agency was actually created by the owner of a large estate. In the case of the new town of Reston, Virginia, thirty miles from the centre of Washington, DC, the first developer (Robert E. Simon Jr.) in 1961 acquired 6,750 acres from a single owner at a cost of $13 million – or an average cost of just under $2,000 per acre. The land was also acquired from a single owner in the cases of Foster City, Leguna Niguel, Rancho Bernardo and Sunset Sacramento – which are all Californian new towns. In the case of Irvine

Ranch, forty miles south of the centre of Los Angeles with a projected population of 300,000, the 93,000 acre estate has been owned by the Irvine family since 1864. The developing agency is also the estate owning family firm in the Californian new towns of Mission Viejo (O'Neill Ranch), and Valencia (Newhall Ranch) and Janss/Conejo (Eichler and Kaplan 1967).

These towns are all developed by private agencies, but in terms of size of development and distance from the cities they serve, and perhaps in some other characteristics, they are comparable to the British new towns discussed in this unit. One major difference however is that the US new towns have not accommodated many members of relatively low income groups. A main point of criticism is that they are high or middle income settlements.

Another vital difference between these private enterprise new towns and those of Britain is that in Britain the developing agencies have the power of compulsory purchase of land. In practice the power of compulsory purchase is a measure of last resort – a public body like a development corporation prefers to acquire through negotiation. But the existence of the power of compulsory purchase includes rules for the valuation of the land, and so provides the framework for negotiations on the price to be paid.

The rules for the valuation of land are determined by the *Land Compensation Act* of 1961. A major principle of valuation is:

… that an acquiring authority shall not pay any increase in the value of land if the increase may be said to be brought about by the scheme of development which gives rise to the need for compulsory purchase. (Heap 1963 p 176)

In other words the development agency in a British new town is given the power to acquire land compulsorily at that price which would have existed if the new town did not exist.

Some provision of this nature is necessary if a public development agency is to be successful in acquiring land at as low cost as it might be acquired by a private developer. A public agency like a new town development corporation has to operate in the open. Approval for the designation of a town including a specification of exactly which land is included in the designated area may well have been laid before Parliament for approval before the development corporation came into existence. There will have been much publicity and public discussion of the plans for the new town. Without some such provision land prices in the designated area and the surrounding area would rocket upwards in anticipation of the growth of the town.

A private development company can by contrast negotiate in secrecy, and if one landowner refuses to sell or asks too much the development company can change its plans about the land it needs. Even so, where land ownership is fragmented a private development agency will probably have to pay much more for land it acquires when its intentions and ambitions are known than it has to for its initial purchases. In the case of the US new town of Columbia in Maryland developed by the Rouse Company, the difficulties of land assembly have been described in these terms:

… The story of Rouse's negotiations with land owners over the next months reads like a James Bond novel; secret rooms, plot strategy, and dummy corporations characterized the process. To reduce the possibility that land owners would become aware of CRD's intention to build a community, Rouse created shell corporations under such names as Serenity Acres, Cedar Farms, and Potomic Estates. Each of the corporations contracted with a different realtor. Their 'separate' activities made it appear that there were several unrelated efforts in the area to establish a number of small-scale subdivisions.

All this behind-the-scenes sleight-of-hand reveals the difficulties of acquiring a large site when ownership is distributed among hundreds of individuals. Moreover, because of its agreement with Connecticut General, CRD was committed to spending no more than an average of $1,500 per acre. In the six-month period between April and October, Rouse dealt with 328 individual owners and made over 140 separate purchases. Strategy was determined on a day by day basis in terms of each piece of property, the personality of the owner, and his financial position. At the end of the six-month period, surprising even itself, CRD was able to announce that its affiliate, the Howard Research and Development Corporation, had secured slightly less than 15,000 acres midway between Baltimore and Washington. Average cost per acre was $1,450. There remained – and still do to this date – five 'holdouts,' totalling 850 acres. (Eichler and Kaplan 1967 p 61)

Compulsory purchase powers can thus be regarded as an institutionalized means of giving to public agencies engaged in new town development what private agencies can mostly achieve in other ways.

The assembly of nearly all the land of the intended site is of course necessary for comprehensive planning. But as the infrastructure of roads, water supply and sewerage facilities is developed, individual building sites or completed buildings can be sold freehold by the development agency or they can be let. A vital element of Ebenezer Howard's original conception of new towns was that the property should be rented:

... Amongst the essential differences between Garden City and other municipalities, one of the chief is its method of raising its revenue. Its entire revenue is derived from rents; and one of the purposes of this work is to show that the rents which may very reasonably be expected from the various tenants on the estate will be amply sufficient, if paid into the coffers of Garden City, (a) to pay the interest on the money with which the estate is purchased, (b) to provide a sinking fund for the purpose of paying off the principal, (c) to construct and maintain all such works as are usually constructed and maintained by municipal and other local authorities out of rates compulsorily levied, and (d) (after redemption of debentures) to provide a large surplus for other people, such as old-age pensions and insurance against accident.

Perhaps no difference between town and country is more noticeable than the difference in the rent charged for the use of the soil. Thus, while in some parts of London the rent is equal to £30,000 an acre, £4 an acre is an extremely high rent for agricultural land. This enormous difference of rental value is, of course, almost entirely due to the presence in the one case and the absence in the other of a large population; and, as it cannot be attributed to the action of any particular individuals, it is frequently spoken of as the 'unearned increment', i.e. unearned by the landlord, though a more correct term would be 'collectively earned increment'.

The presence of a considerable population thus giving a greatly additional value to the soil, it is obvious that a migration of population on any considerable scale to any particular area will be certainly attended with a corresponding rise in the value of the land so settled upon, and it is also obvious that such increment of value may, with some foresight and pre-arrangement, become the property of the migrating people. (Howard 1965 edition pp 58–9)

This idea was more or less carried through in Britain's new towns until the late 1960s. For the first two decades after the passing of the New Towns Act in 1946 only about one in every five dwellings in the new towns were sold for owner occupation. Four out of every five dwellings were let directly to the tenants with the development corporation acting as landlord. The current policy is that 50 per cent of all houses should be sold to their occupiers and only 50 per cent shall remain in the rented sector. Most of the industrial and commercial property is also owned by the development corporation and leased to the occupiers, and this kind of property has so far provided the best financial returns:

> ... It is on the industrial and commercial success of a town that a development corporation has mainly to rely for any profit. It takes time for values to build up – particularly shop values, which are so dependent on the rate of population increase; but once the shopping and industrial areas are firmly established, values can rise remarkably quickly. Even then the corporation may not be able to collect this increase until leases fall due for renewal or rents can be recalculated under a review clause. Leases vary in their terms, but for industrial and commercial buildings leases of up to twenty-one years are usual, with reviews at the seventh and fourteenth year. In the case of ground leases the period is much longer, and until recently it was normal estate practice to have a fixed ground rent with no provision for review. In the new towns, with their rapidly rising land-values, this was soon seen to be unsatisfactory and the development corporations pioneered a new practice, now widely adopted, of rising ground rents or a review at various times during the lease. (Schaffer 1972 edition p 213)

Private agencies developing new towns do not usually retain ownership of property. Perhaps the underlying reason for this is the difficulty of securing enough capital for a long enough period. In the cases of Letchworth and Welwyn Garden City the developing companies did retain ownership of most of the property, but these towns grew at rates which would nowadays be considered very slow. In the case of new towns in the United States the developing company expects to sell all the houses and depends upon the sale of houses to make the venture financially viable.

The combination of the purchase of land at relatively low cost and the retention of ownership of most of the property by the development corporation is probably an essential element for the achievement of social balance as far as accommodating members of low income groups is concerned. It is an unfortunate fact that even in advanced industrial societies only a proportion of the population can afford the cost of a new house. It is usually estimated that in Britain, for example, although half of existing households own their homes, only about a quarter of the population can afford to buy a new house *out of income*. (This kind of estimate is based upon what building societies are prepared to lend.) In the United States the corresponding proportion has been estimated at a half (Clawson 1971 p 321). As far as rented accommodation is concerned what people can afford to pay in rent depends upon what proportion of income it is considered reasonable that people should devote to housing. In practice the rent of new houses outside the public sector is of the same order of magnitude as the repayments for a 90 or 100 per cent mortgage.

Accommodating a significant proportion of members of low income groups depends therefore on subsidies of some kind. Part of this subsidy in Britain comes from governmental sources as can be illustrated even from the early history of Letchworth:

> ... The demand for workers cottages was still not fully met, for many more of the cheaper dwellings were needed than the co-partnership was willing to build, and the garden city company itself promoted a company, called Letchworth Cottages and Buildings Ltd, for the purpose. The capital of this company was subject to a dividend of 4 per cent, guaranteed by the parent company, and was raised independently from people interested in good housing, including the directors themselves. It was able to borrow from the Public Works Loan Board, at 3.5 per cent interest, one-half the cost of building for a period of thirty years, which in practice worked out at less than half the actual cost, because the Board always undervalued, to keep on the safe side! This company's cottages were let at rents of from 4s 3d to 6s 9d per week, inclusive

of rates. After the passing of the Housing Act of 1909, which enabled loans to be granted on special terms to public utility societies, other societies were formed to take advantage of these loans and to build the cottages for which there was a constant demand. Before the first war the average cost of a cottage at Letchworth containing living-room, scullery and three bedrooms, including drainage, fencing, etc., complete (everything except the land), was a little over £150, and it was let at a renting including rates of 5s 6d per week. A cottage with a parlour was let at about 1s per week more. Even at these rents the lowest paid labourer could not be housed, and as the garden city was intended for all classes of the community, the poor as well as the well-paid workman, there was a strong desire to build cottages that the very poorest labourer could afford to rent. The garden city company's subsidiary cottage company did what it could, but could not borrow money on such favourable terms as the local authority, so that the Hitchin Rural District Council, within whose area the garden city came, was induced experimentally to build four cottages at a total cost of £560 for the four, which were let at 4s 6d per week each, including rates, and showed a small balance in favour of the council. This was possible because the local authority could borrow the whole of the capital cost for a period up to sixty years; while a public utility society could borrow no more than two-thirds of the valuation of the cottages built (and valuation was invariably under cost) for a period not exceeding forty years. The rural district council afterwards built a further six small cottages, and later on a scheme of a hundred. This was at a time when house building by local authorities was something of a novelty, so that the rural district council's schemes showed much enterprise and some belief in the garden city. (Purdom 1949 p 65)

Part of the subsidy comes from other property owned by the development agency, as can be illustrated from the Welwyn Garden City even in its prewar history as a private enterprise new town:

... The ground-rents at Welwyn are fixed at what is considered to be their market value – that is, at the highest figure that can be obtained. Sites are taken on their merits and the ground-rent is a fixed sum – there is not one price for one man and a different price for another. The advantage that the town has to offer in the way of good planning, a well-considered scheme of development, low rates, and the general amenities of the district are taken into account. No attempt has been made to dispose of land in large blocks at low rents, though sites for a number of houses at the beginning were let to public utility societies for a lower figure than would have been charged for the plots separately; but this practice has been discontinued. No land is disposed of except for immediate building. There has been no opportunity, therefore, for speculation. The earlier rents were lower than the later rents, and the tendency, as already noted, is for a gradual rise, which is to the advantage of existing lessees.

Land for workmen's cottages is disposed of at a figure which will enable the cottages to be let at the lowest possible rent. The highest market price is not sought for this land, as it is considered to be in the company's interest, that is to say the interest of the scheme as a garden city providing for the industrial population, that every encouragement should be given to the building of workmen's houses. (Purdom 1949 p 337)

The new towns built since 1946 have depended partly on both these kinds of subsidy in accommodating members of relatively low income groups. New Town Development Corporations received a subsidy from the central government for rented dwellings of the same kind as is received by local authorities for council housing for rent. As the quotation from Schaffer has already illustrated, letting other kinds of property has been profitable and so has contributed, albeit very indirectly, to the cost of providing workers' housing. But perhaps the major contribution to the financial viability of the new towns of the 1940s has been the general inflation of property values.

Land was acquired in the earlier postwar period at a cost measured in terms of hundreds of pounds per acre. Houses were built in the early postwar period at a cost of £2,000 or so. At the time of writing, the cost of residential building land is measured in terms of tens of thousands of pounds per acre and there are not many places in Britain where an average new house can be bought for less than £10,000. The new town development corporations, like all other property companies, have benefited financially from these generally soaring prices, as well as gaining the benefit from the increase in values which is attributable to their own town building activities. These financial benefits have helped the new towns to provide housing for many people who could not otherwise afford to buy or rent a new house.

With a generous usage of the definitional characteristics suggested in this section Britain has, as illustrated in Table 2, twenty-two satellite new towns. Up to the end of 1972 their total population had increased by 600,000 since designation. These twenty-two new towns have plans which envisage an ultimate population of two and a half millions.

Table 2 Satellite new towns in the United Kingdom

	Year of designation	Population at time of designation	Population 1972	Ultimate population
London's new towns:			(thousands)	
Stevenage	1946	7	73	100-105
Crawley	1947	9	69	85
Hemel Hempstead	1947	21	73	80
Harlow	1947	5	80	undecided
Welwyn Garden City	1948	19	42	50
Hatfield	1948	9	26	30
Basildon	1949	25	82	134
Bracknell	1949	5	38	60
Milton Keynes	1967	40	50	250
Peterborough	1967	81	91	187
Northampton	1968	131	138	260
Total London's new towns		352	762	1,200 (approx.)
Glasgow's new towns:				
East Kilbride	1947	2	67	90-100
Cumbernauld	1955	2	35	100
Livingston	1962	2	18	100
Irvine	1966	35	44	120
Total Glasgow's new towns		42	164	410-430
Liverpool's new towns:				
Skelmersdale	1961	10	34	80
Runcorn	1964	30	44	100
Birmingham's new towns:				
Redditch	1964	32	44	90
Telford	1968	73	87	250
Belfast's new towns:				
Craigavon	1965	61	73	180
Antrim	1966	33	40	74
Ballymena	1967	48	50	96
Grand total		680	1,298	2,500 (approx.)

Notes: This table covers developments under the New Towns Act managed by development corporations appointed by the central government.

There is no absolute distinction between satellite and other new towns. The table covers towns which are expected to gain most of their population from the five major cities listed. Other new towns or places which have been designated as new towns are Aycliffe, Corby, Peterlee, Warrington, Washington, Glenrothes and Londonderry.

Source: Town and Country Planning, January 1973

4 Howard's proposals and British new town policy

Extracts from the New Towns Act 1946:

... 1 (1) If the Minister is satisfied, after consultation with any local authorities who appear to him to be concerned, that it is expedient in the national interest that any area of land should be developed as a new town by a corporation established under this Act, he may make an order designating that area as the site of the proposed new town ...

2 (1) For the purposes of the development of each new town the site of which is designated under section one of this Act, the Minister shall by order establish a corporation (hereinafter called a development corporation) consisting of a chairman, a deputy chairman and such number of other members, not exceeding seven, as may be prescribed by the order; and every such corporation shall be a body corporate by such name as may be prescribed by the order, with perpetual succession and a common seal and power to hold land without licence in mortmain.

2 (2) The objects of a development corporation established for the purposes of a new town shall be to secure the laying out and development of the new town in accordance with proposals approved in that behalf under the following provisions of this Act, and for that purpose every such corporation shall have power to acquire, hold, manage and dispose of land and other property, to carry out building and other operations, to provide water, electricity, gas, sewerage and other services, to carry on any business or undertaking in or for the purposes of the new town, and generally to do anything necessary or expedient for the purposes of the new town or for purposes incidental thereto:

Provided that, subject to the provision of this Act with respect to the making of advances to development corporations, a development corporation shall not have power to borrow money.

The new towns envisaged in the Reith Reports and the New Towns Act of 1946 differ in a number of important ways from the scheme put forward by Ebenezer Howard. Perhaps the most important single difference is that members of the development corporation are appointed by, and are responsible to, the central government. The development corporation is allowed to borrow money only from the government and the corporation returns to the central government any profits it makes. Members of the development corporations may well be 'gentlemen of undoubted honour and probity' as Howard suggested for the members of his new town trusts, but they are not in any way formally responsible to the population of the area for which they serve.

One reason for the 'independent' status of the development corporation is the fact that in a number of places the designation of the new town was strongly opposed by the existing residents of the locality. This opposition was particularly strong at the first new town to be designated at Stevenage. When Lewis Silkin, Minister of Town and Country Planning, visited old Stevenage in 1946 he was greeted with cries of Gestapo! Dictator! The tyres of his car were let down and sand put in the petrol tank. The name boards on the railway station were replaced with ones marked 'Silkingrad' (see Orlans 1952 pp 60-7).

It could therefore be convincingly argued that the new towns programme would have been stunted from the start if the development corporation were democratically accountable to the existing population of the area. It could further be argued that such accountability would in any case be unjustified because the new town was designed to serve the incoming population not the existing population. Perhaps considerations of these kinds were uppermost in the minds of the authors of the 1946 Act. Certainly that Act gave power to the minister to wind up the development corporation and hand over the assets to the local authority and it was envisaged that this would happen as the new town approached maturity. In fact this provision was repealed by the 1959 New Towns Act which established the New Town Commission – a national body with members appointed by the minister in the same way as members of a development corporation – which in the early 1960s took over the assets of the four new towns (Crawley, Hemel Hempstead, Welwyn Garden City and Hatfield) which were at that time envisaged as being near to their ultimate size.

The reason given for this amendment was that it was undesirable on social grounds for a local authority to own almost all the properties in their area and was outside the function of elected authorities. J. R. Bevins, Parliamentary Secretary to the Minister of Housing at that time, stated that 'Estate management should be stable and it is unwise to mix it with politics' (see Schaffer 1972 pp 215–7 for more details). It is up to you to speculate on the validity of this line of argument.

A quite different kind of governmental machinery exists for 'new towns' built under the 1952 Town Development Act. This act allowed for the expansion of small towns through agreement between the *exporting* authority and the *receiving* authority. Thus London has agreements with thirty-two different local authorities. Glasgow has forty-three such agreements, and Birmingham has fifteen. In many cases these town development schemes (or expanded town schemes as they are often called) are very small involving the construction of only a few hundred dwellings. Sometimes these expanded town schemes involve little more than the construction of new dormitory suburbs in the administrative area of a local authority neighbouring the city. But in a number of cases expanded town schemes are on much the same scale as developments under the New Town Acts and fall within the definition of satellite new towns suggested in the previous section of this unit (see Table 3).

Table 3 Selected town expansion schemes of a satellite character in England

	Exporting/receiving authority	Dwellings for letting		
		Completed by 30.6.72	To be built	Total
London's schemes:	Andover M B	1,974	4,026	6,000
	Ashford U D	1,953	2,297	4,250
	Aylesbury M B	2,182	1,518	3,700
	Basingstoke M B	5,428	3,822	9,250
	Bletchley U D	4,240	760	5,000
	Bury St Edmunds M B	1,204	1,796	3,000
	Haverhill U D	2,517	1,983	4,500
	Kings Lynn M B	1,324	2,176	3,500
	Swindon	7,915	585	8,500
	Thetford M B	2,590	410	3,000
	Wellingborough U D	2,204	7,796	10,000
	Witham U D	1,747	1,253	3,000
Birmingham's schemes:	Daventry	1,529	3,746	5,275
	Tamworth M B	2,804	3,696	6,500
Liverpool's schemes:	Ellesmere Port M B	2,383	3,117	5,500
	Widnes M B	853	3,307	4,160
	Winsford U D	2,627	4,039	6,666
Manchester's schemes:	Burnley C B	14	2,686	2,700
	Crewe M B	43	3,957	4,000
Newcastle upon Tyne's schemes:	Seaton Valley U D (Cramlington)	892	5,608	6,500
	Longbenton U D (Killingworth)	1,360	2,657	4,017

Notes: 1 This table covers expansion schemes agreed in accordance with the 1952 Town Development Act where the development is managed by agreement between the exporting and receiving authority. The table covers most agreements involving the construction of 3,000 or more dwellings for letting. There is often a substantial amount of house construction for sale also associated with most of these schemes but the local authority does not usually play any special role in this area.
2 Burnley also has agreements with Liverpool and London for 2,200 and 700 dwellings respectively.

Source: Town and Country Planning, January 1973

The central government contributes to the finance for expanded town schemes through housing subsidies and grants for water supply and sewerage facilities.

But the expansion is planned and controlled by agreement between the exporting and receiving authorities. The receiving authority can act as developer and can retain ownership of as much of the developed property as it can afford to finance. Those receiving authorities which have retained ownership have no doubt profited financially to the benefit of all their ratepayers. But the extent to which expanded towns have in practice become property owning democracies, in the spirit of *Howard's* ideas, is not clear.

Another major difference between Howard's proposals and Britain's new towns is in size. The size range proposed by the New Towns Committee was 20–60,000.

. . . In the First Interim Report we said that preliminary consideration of the appropriate size of new towns had led to a figure of from 20,000 to 60,000, subject to exceptions either way. Uniformity in size and cultural pattern is undesirable and we do not suggest any one figure within this range for general application.

Factors which govern the upper limit of this range include:
1 Dwellings should be within walking or cycling distance of the industrial zones and shopping and cultural centres, thus minimizing the need for local transport.
2 Contact with the countryside is essential; the country should be within reasonably easy reach of the centre.
3 It is difficult to attain a sense of civic consciousness and unit in very large towns.
4 As most new town projects are likely to be started while the demand for housing will still be very great, speed in creation will be a primary objective.

Several medium-sized new towns at a reasonable distance from the conurbation whose congestion they have to relieve can be built more quickly than a smaller number of larger towns. An important factor will be the availability of workers, and it would be more difficult to draw them from a conurbation to one or two large new towns than to several smaller towns. Difficulties of transport and accommodation would add considerably to the cost. If the projects be within reach of the outer rim of the big pools of labour it will make for speed and economy in building. This, incidentally, is one reason why peripheral suburban spread is so hard to resist. (Ministry of Town and Country Planning, *Final Report of the New Towns Committee*, p 8)

The original designations were mostly within this proposed range, but as the new town programme got underway and as the projections of Britain's future population were revised upwards – so were the designated populations of the new towns. Instead of creating clusters of small new towns, as Howard had advocated, the designated populations of existing towns were increased. As you can see if you look back to Table 2 most of the new towns now plan for ultimate populations within the range of 100–250,000. Apart from the fact that such projected expansions seem very practicable, there does not appear to be any explicit justification for this change of policy except for rather vague arguments about the establishment of 'counter-magnets' to London's growth. You should consider this question again when you study Unit 27, 'Optimum size of cities'.

A third major difference between Howard's proposals and Britain's new towns is that there is no provision for association of the towns with nearby agricultural activities (except in so far as allotments are provided in the town). This factor, coupled with the larger size of the new towns, means that they miss out on the presumed advantages of the country segment of the town-country pole. As far as access to the countryside is concerned the new towns do not differ from most other urban settlements in Britain. Widespread changes in the character of the British countryside may however have made the idea of a

Figure 5 Britain's new and expanded satellite towns Note: The map shows only those new and expanded towns listed in Tables 2 and 3

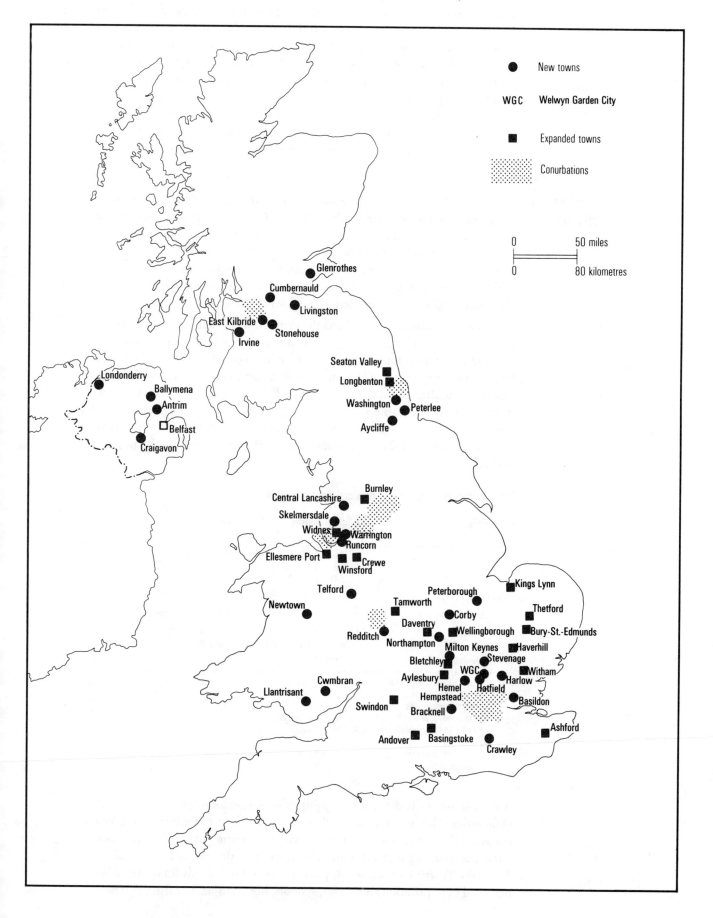

town-country blend increasingly irrelevant. The uses of land surrounding the new towns, like that of other agricultural land, have undergone radical changes since the beginning of the century and in particular since the Second World War. Hedges have been ploughed up to create vast fields and miles of footpaths have become nothing more than dotted lines on the Ordnance Survey maps as farm mechanization and specialization have replaced the traditional mixed farming and permanent pasture. On the other hand the lack of any association with agriculture also means that the new towns miss out on any possibilities of any special contribution to the solution of environmental and resource problems through the use of town wastes for agricultural purposes.

5 Self-containment and social balance

The phrase 'self-contained and balanced communities' which set the tone of the terms of reference of the New Towns Committee is extremely rich and ambiguous in its meanings. The significance of ambiguities, particularly in the context of 'community' will be considered in Section 6. The concern of this section is the nature of some of the meanings of the adjectives 'self-contained' and 'balanced' together with a discussion of the extent to which the new towns have achieved the aims implied in these adjectives.

Self-containment

The adjective 'self-contained' has three meanings. First it refers just to physical factors. The new towns were in part a reaction against scattered forms of urban development such as the ribbon development of the interwar period, and the sites were chosen to avoid as far as possible the use of high quality agricultural land. The designated areas of new towns are compact in form. As shown in Table 4 they also use less land per head of population than towns of similar size, but they use more land per head of population than county boroughs, and no doubt much more than that used by the populations of their parent cities.

Table 4 Provisions of land for new and existing towns

Urban category		Housing*	Industry	Open space	Education	Total urban area
		ha/1,000 population (acres/1,000 population)				
County boroughs (79)	a	7.6(18.8)	1.4(3.5)	3.3(8.1)	0.5(1.2)	17.5(43.3)
	b	9.5(23.4)	2.0(5.0)	4.2(10.5)	1.3(3.3)	21.6(53.4)
Earlier new towns (15)	b	10.9(26.9)	2.1(5.3)	4.4(11.0)	1.9(4.6)	22.2(55.0)
Recent new towns (9)	b	8.6(21.3)	3.5(8.6)	6.9(17.1)	1.7(4.3)	24.5(60.5)
Large town map	a	12.6(31.2)	2.3(5.7)	6.1(15.1)	1.0(2.6)	29.8(73.6)
areas ø (186)	b	14.7(36.3)	2.9(7.2)	6.1(15.2)	2.1(5.2)	32.8(81.1)
Small settlements† (260)	a	27.4(67.8)‡	1.2(3.0)	4.0(9.8)	0.7(1.7)	34.6(85.5)

Notes: a Existing situation (c. 1950, except for small settlements)
       b Proposed situation
       * Net residential area
       ø Large towns, of over 10,000 population, which are not county boroughs
       † Under 10,000 population, ie small towns and villages (c. 1960)
       ‡ Including commercial land
       Figures in brackets in the first column indicate number of settlements in sample
Source: Best 1972

A second but quite different meaning of *self-contained* relates to the provision of facilities. The new towns could not hope, because of their size, to provide urban facilities on the scale that are available in the parent city, but they were intended to provide facilities for the day to day use of their inhabitants. The New Towns Committee Reports proposed standards (in terms of facilities per head of population) for shops, schools, hospitals and health centres, theatres, concert halls and libraries. They also proposed that there should be maternity and child welfare clinics, family and child guidance clinics, restaurants and of course public houses.

The Development Corporations accepted this aspect of self-containment as an aim, but there is nothing in the New Towns Act which *required* them to provide these facilities. Responsibility for providing facilities such as schools, normally the responsibility of the local authorities, are also the responsibility of the local authorities in new towns. The new towns are by most standards well provided with schools but partly because of the young immigrant population they are often inadequate in size in relation to the pupil populations. It does not help matters that the provision of most kinds of local authority facility is the responsibility of the county councils, most of whose ratepayers do not live in the new town. In the early years new town development imposes a significant extra burden on the rates.

In the case of facilities which must be provided by private enterprise such as shops it is impossible to ensure provision in advance of demand. Retail organizations depend upon current takings not future demand for their profits. When shops do come they enjoy a fairly monopolistic position. Residents of the new town complain both of lack of choice and high prices.

In the case of other facilities, such as cinemas, the situation may be worsened because on a national scale patrons are being diverted to other forms of entertainment. For the private investor in most cases risks in investing in the building of a new cinema outweigh potential gains. The result is that new towns are often bereft of such entertainment (the argument applies even more forcibly to theatres) for many years. In Stevenage, for example, a new town with a population of 70,000, there is still no cinema twenty-seven years after designation, although the authors are reliably informed that one is now being built.

The difficulties of getting public facilities in new towns is nowhere better illustrated than at Aycliffe in County Durham, which though hardly classifiable as a satellite town (the population has been drawn largely from the surrounding mining villages) was established as a greenfields site without any existing urban nucleus apart from an industrial trading estate.

. . . The fact that Newton Aycliffe started from scratch means a complete absence of community facilities. Every other new town had some start, even if it was only a couple of public houses as at Peterlee, but Aycliffe's only asset was its proximity to Darlington. By 1954 the population was nearly 5,000 but there were still no public buildings or community facilities. The Corporation and an energetic Community Association made persistent efforts to persuade private developers to build a cinema and to persuade the Local Education Authority to participate in a joint scheme for an assembly hall and other communal buildings as part of the secondary school. But in both cases the negotiations were unfruitful. In 1959 the Development Corporation reported that they were building homes for the parents of residents, partly with the objective of discouraging the 'general week-end exodus of young families visiting their home town'.

There were also some successes. An over sixties club was completed in 1959 with aid from a charity, and the next year a working men's club was built with money from the Northern Federation of Breweries. The Corporation reviewed the needs for social facilities and sent a list to the Ministry. In first place came a youth centre, and in second place a town assembly hall. At that time the population was just under 11,000. Newton Aycliffe did not get its youth centre until 1967 when the population was 18,000. (Thomas 1969b pp 892–3)

In so far as the adjective *self-contained* relates to the provision of facilities its meaning relates solely to the physical characteristic of new towns. A third related meaning of *self-contained* has behavioural overtones. The aim was to provide a full range of facilities for day to day use. But it was also assumed that this provision would lead to the residents of the town satisfying their day to day needs within the town rather than by travelling to other areas. This assumption was made at a time when only about one in every twenty households possessed a car. It is not so easy to make a quarter of a century later when something like two-thirds of households in new towns have at least one car.

This particular aspect of new town development as far as journeys to work in London's New Towns is concerned has been described as follows:

... Self-containment can, of course, only be a matter of degree. It is unrealistic to expect that the local facilities should meet all of the requirements of all of the residents all of the time. The idea of a self-contained community is in fact more like a wish than a goal. It is like wishing a young couple a successful marriage. Whether or not the wish is fulfilled depends primarily upon the reaction of the couple to each other. But it also depends upon other factors such as their reaction to other people and perhaps upon the quantity of worldly goods they can command. There is generally little the wellwisher can do to ensure success.

In the same way there is little the Development Corporation of a new town can do to ensure self-containment. The corporation can have only an indirect influence on the decisions made by individuals as to whether to use the facilities within the town, or to travel to other areas to satisfy their needs and tastes. But there is a great deal the development corporations can do to make self-containment possible – such as matching the levels of population and employment. And there is a great deal the development corporation can do to encourage self-containment – such as providing the environment and amenities which will induce the people who work in the town to live there too. (Thomas 1969a p 382)

... The procedures followed for making housing available mean that the large majority of those who take jobs in a new town also move their homes to the town. As far as journeys to work are concerned a high degree of self-containment is built into the new towns.

Even at this stage there are exceptions. If they live within a reasonable distance, new and existing employees of firms moving to the new towns may prefer to commute rather than change their place of residence. Some employees may buy a house in a nearby village rather than in the town itself. It can be expected that there will also be some lack of support for the self-containment idea from those who do move to the town. The head of the household has to have a job in the town, but this constraint does not apply to other members of his family.

With the passage of time it may be expected that the self-containment principle might be further eroded. There is nothing to prevent heads of households taking new jobs outside once they have secured accommodation within the town. As the children grow the housewife may seek a job and she need not limit herself to the opportunities available in the town. When the sons and daughters are older they, too, will be looking for work, and it may well be that the interest and variety of employment available in London attracts them more than the possibility of a short journey to work.

As the family grows older it may become more affluent and ambitious. Life in a town dominated by public housing may cease to be attractive, and there may be a move to what is considered a more desirable area, even when members of the family continue to work in the town.

All of these trends would make the new towns less self-contained. The growth trends in the new towns can be viewed as tug-of-war between trends of this kind and the self-containment which is built in to each accretion of population and employment. The results of the tug-of-war can be gauged by comparing the growth of journeys within the new towns with the growth of journeys to and from them.

. . . to add precision to the discussion, a special terminology will be used. Journeys within a town will be called *local journeys*. The sum of journeys by residents to a town who work outside and journeys by those employed in a town and living outside will be called *crossing journeys*. The ratio of local to crossing journeys will be called the *index of commuting independence* or independence index for short. The independence index is a measure of the extent to which a town is self-contained with regard to journeys to work. The higher the value of the index the more self-contained the town.

Table 5 gives independence indices for each of the new towns for 1951, 1961 and 1966. The pattern of change in the different towns has been remarkably similar. Over 1951 to 1961 six of the eight new towns became more self-contained. The exceptions were Hatfield and Welwyn Garden City. The average independence index increased from 0.85 to 1.33. The growth of self-containment of Basildon and Stevenage is particularly striking. The independence index for these towns more than doubled over the decade.

Table 5 Indices of commuting independence for London's new towns in 1951, 1961 and 1966

Town	1951	1961	1966
	(Ratio of local to crossing journeys)		
Harlow	1.42	2.04	2.05
Stevenage	.92	2.29	2.03
Hemel Hempstead M B [1]	1.31	1.82	1.72
Crawley	.98	1.59	1.58
Welwyn Garden City	1.12	1.09	1.12
Bracknell	.90	1.13	1.02
Basildon	.36	.96	.96
Hatfield R D [2]	.65	.63	.66
Average (weighted)	.85	1.33	1.33

Notes: 1   Some parts of Hemel Hempstead Municipal Borough, which include several factories, lie outside the designated area of the New Town. The independence indices for the New Town area are .80, 1.38 and 1.42 respectively, lower than for the M B.
2   One of the main functions of Hatfield New Town was to provide housing for the De Havilland Aircraft Works (now Hawker Siddeley Aviation and Hawker Siddeley Dynamics) which lie outside the designated area. It seems preferable therefore to use figures relating to Hatfield Rural District, which includes the new town and the industrial centre it was designed to serve, although the R D also includes a substantial amount of other employment and population and covers a much wider area.

Over 1961 to 1966 the degree of self-containment did not change very much. There was a fall in the independence index for Bracknell, Crawley, Hemel Hempstead and Stevenage, and in the other four towns the index increased slightly or did not change significantly. The difference between the pattern of change over 1951–61 and 1961–6 is noteworthy. Part of this difference may be attributable to the fact that in 1951 the growth of the new towns had scarcely got under way. The pattern of journeys in that year relates mainly to the original population of the designated areas. The dramatic changes for the period 1951–61 are in most cases a reflection of a change in the nature as well as of the growth of these areas in terms of population and employment. Welwyn Garden City and Hemel Hempstead were established towns in 1951, but the remainder of the new towns were mixtures in varying degree of sleepy village, market town, and dormitory suburb or exurb. By 1961 they were all bustling urban nuclei, already developing their own traffic problems.

The pattern of change of journeys in the new towns is fairly uniform, but there are substantial differences between the various towns with regard to the relative number of local and crossing journeys. The degree of self-containment is not at all uniform, and the differences have tended to persist as the new towns have grown. In 1951 Harlow, Hemel Hempstead and Welwyn Garden City were the most self-contained of the new towns, but it seems the factors involved were rather different in each case. Harlow was self-contained because it was isolated; Hemel Hempstead because it was well established; Welwyn because it was already a major centre for employment as well as population. Basildon and Hatfield were the least self-contained – both were predominantly residential areas.

In 1966 the new towns fell naturally into two groups. Four of the five largest are the most self-contained: Harlow, Stevenage, Crawley and Hemel Hempstead. Of the remainder Welwyn Garden City and Hatfield have hardly changed with regard to self-containment. Their proximity to each other and to London helps to explain this trend. Both Bracknell and in particular Basildon have become more self-contained but they are still much less self-contained than Harlow or Stevenage.

Before we go on to examine more systematically some of the factors which have influenced this pattern of change, let us see what this independence index means in practice. Take, for example, Stevenage: one of the most self-contained of the new towns. In 1966 there were just over 26,000 residents in employment in Stevenage. Twenty-two thousand of them worked in the town and the other 4,000 worked outside. Those who worked outside did not do so because of lack of employment opportunities in the town. The level of employment in Stevenage in 1966 was 29,000, so there was a healthy employment surplus. In fact most of the journeys crossing the boundaries of Stevenage were not made by residents – and this is a feature which, as will be seen, is fairly characteristic of the new towns – but were made by people from other areas travelling to Stevenage to work. In this case the number of daily journeys into the town is nearly 7,000.

The flow of commuting in and out of the new towns is influenced by a variety of factors. The flow depends upon the proximity of the town to other urban concentrations, and it depends upon the availability of transport facilities of all kinds – cars and roads, trains, buses and bicycles. The nearer a town to other centres of employment, and the easier it is to travel, the greater the likelihood that residents will take work outside. The nearer the town to other residential areas the easier it is for people to work in the town without living in it.

The number of journeys in and out of a town also depends upon the level of employment relative to the number of residents in employment within the town. If there is a surplus of employment some workers travel from other areas. If there is a deficit of employment some residents must find work outside the town. Imbalances of this kind represent the minimum need for commuting into or out of a town.

The conventional way of comparing the levels of employment and population is to use the *job ratio* as a measure. The job ratio is the employment level in a town divided by the number of residents in employment in the area and expressed as a percentage. When there is an employment surplus the job ratio is more than 100. When there is an employment deficit the job ratio is less than 100. When the job ratio equals 100 the town may be said to be balanced with regard to the levels of employment and population – though of course the town may lack balance in other ways.

Table 6 gives job ratios for the new towns in 1951, 1961 and 1966. No clear pattern is apparent. Six out of eight new towns were net importers of labour in 1951. Five out of eight were net importers in 1966. Bracknell has become more imbalanced – the job ratio of 108 in 1951 had increased to 126 in 1966 – making Bracknell the least balanced of all the new towns on this measure. Basildon and Hatfield have steadily become more balanced. The large employment deficit in Basildon in 1951 had been

Table 6 Job ratios in London's new towns in 1951, 1961 and 1966

Town	1951	1961	1966
	(ratio of employment to residents in employment as a percentage)		
Bracknell	108	115	126
Basildon	37	82	107
Crawley	112	101	111
Hatfield R D	123	107	96
Harlow	98	86	97
Hemel Hempstead M B	101	96	97
Stevenage	124	109	112
Welwyn Garden City	124	125	122
Average (weighted)	100	100	107

converted into a small surplus by 1966. Hatfield has become more balanced in the other direction. The main purpose of the town was to provide housing for the workers of the de Havilland Aircraft factory, and the employment surplus in the area in 1951 had been changed to a small deficit by 1966.

In the other five new towns the changes in the job ratio haven't been very large. In most of them there has been a persistence of the position in 1951. Welwyn Garden City, Crawley and Stevenage have continued as employment centres. Harlow and Hemel Hempstead have continued with more or less balanced growth.

Not surprising there are strong relationships between the degree of balance and the extent to which a town is self-contained. Basildon, for example, was the least balanced in 1951 and was also the least self-contained. The four most self-contained towns in 1966 (Harlow, Stevenage, Hemel Hempstead and Crawley) are also among the most balanced. But the relationship doesn't necessarily work the other way round. A balance in the levels of population and employment is a necessary not a sufficient condition for self-containment. Hatfield and Basildon, for example, were both fairly balanced in 1966, but they are the least self-contained of the new towns. (Thomas 1969a pp 392–6)

Figure 6 Index of commuting independence for towns in south east England in 1966 by distance from central London Source: Thomas (1969)

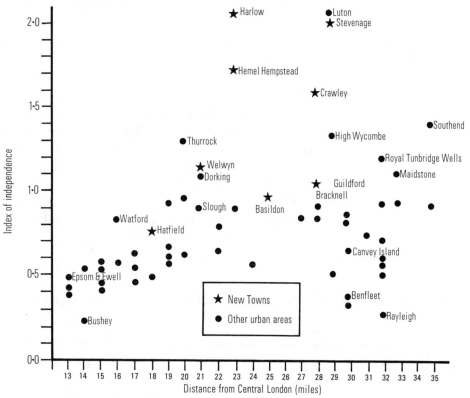

Note: The distance of an area from Central London is taken as the airline distance from Charing Cross to the approximate centre of the area in a whole no. of miles

... There are no towns within 35 miles of central London with a population of less than 150,000 which are as self-contained as Harlow, Stevenage, Hemel Hempstead or Crawley. Only a small proportion of other towns are as self-contained as Basildon, Bracknell or Welwyn Garden City. Only Hatfield of the new towns is typical of other towns in the extent to which it is self-contained. (Thomas 1969a p 404)

The conclusion that the new towns have achieved a certain level of self-containment relative to other places around London is tempered by several considerations. One is the point already mentioned that as the new towns become more established more of the initial immigrants will change either their place of residence or their place of work. In the sense that the offering of a 'package deal' has raised the level of self-containment to a level above the level that will probably be sustained over a long period, an artificially high level of self-containment has been attained. Between 1961 and 1966 the level of self-containment in the London new towns was only just maintained as Table 5 shows. Further, the recent policy of encouraging the sale of development corporation dwellings to tenants in new towns to raise the level of owner occupation nearer to the national average of fifty per cent of dwellings is likely to decrease self-containment. This is because houses thus sold will be taken out of the control of development corporations and may eventually fall into the hands, if not already in the hands, of those working outside the town. By contrast, houses which the development corporations retain can be relet when vacated on the same basis as those newly built, that is to say to those with a job in the town.

One of the disadvantages in a measure such as the index of commuting independence is that, in giving overall measure of self-containment by combining inward and outward journeys, much of what is happening is masked. A comparison of London's new towns with towns similarly placed in relation to London will make this point clearer. Six out of eight of London's new towns are within the range of 20–30 miles from central London. The other two, Hatfield and Welwyn Garden City are somewhat nearer, being 18 and 20 miles respectively from the centre. If one looks at municipal boroughs, county boroughs and urban districts at roughly the same distance from London, a pattern emerges for balance of population and employment (see Table 7).

The contrast between the new towns and those listed in Table 7 is not a simple one since although the largest category of urban areas at this distance from London can be described as 'dormitories' (category A in Table 7), there are also other types of settlement, those balanced in respect of population and employment and employment centres. The features which in 1966 distinguished the new towns from the great majority of places in the Outer Metropolitan Area was their relative independence from London and their relative lack of influence so far on their hinterlands (see also Ogilvy 1968). The former fact makes for a low volume of commuting to London and the latter for a low volume of commuting from surrounding areas compared with other

Table 7 Job ratios for urban local authority areas 20–30 miles from central London, excluding new towns, in 1966

Employment/population balance	Dormitory areas		Balanced	Employment centres	
Range of job ratios	84.9 or below	85.0-94.9	95.0-104.9	105.0-114.9	115.0 or over
Number of towns	14	3	4	2	6
Towns	Benfleet, Berkhamstead, Canvey Island, Chesham, Dorking, Eton, Gravesend, Harpenden, Marlow, New Windsor, Sawbridgeworth, Southborough, Ware, Woking.	Beaconsfield, Bishops Stortford, Tonbridge.	East Grinstead, Frimley and Camberley, Maidenhead, Sevenoaks.	Luton, Thurrock.	Chatham, Chelmsford, Guildford, High Wycombe, Rochester, Slough.

Source: Calculations based on data from Thomas (1969a)

places. In both cases the effect is to tend to decrease the index of commuting independence by minimizing the number of crossing journeys (see Thomas 1969a quoted above).

Relative independence from London for the eight new towns has largely been achieved through the control of allocating houses only to those who had a job in the town. Relative independence from surrounding areas is probably a result of the way in which the towns have grown with employers moving with large proportions of their existing employees and with priority being given in jobs advertised to those living in London. It is likely that independence from London (relative to other places in the Outer Metropolitan Area) will be reduced by the sort of diminution in control, described earlier in this section, which occurs with passage of time and increasing sales of development corporation houses. It is also likely that, in time, the new towns as areas of balanced population and employment or employment centres will become more attractive as places to work in for people living in surrounding areas.

In general terms self-containment was considered an essential factor in helping to create the identity of places; the fear was that unless new towns were balanced for housing and employment, and people encouraged to live and work in the same place, the new towns would become dormitories for neighbouring employment centres. Rather than become dormitories the London new towns are likely themselves to become centres for their surrounding areas (see Ogilvy 1971).

In terms of the reduction of congestion in London the new towns must have had some impact since persuading a number of employers, representing a certain volume of employment, to move out of the city, whatever the decisions of their individual employees at the time, will have the long term net effect of reducing employment in the city and thus also journeys to work in the city. However it must be recognized that the new towns themselves are new centres and as such their attraction for their hinterlands may generate a certain volume of daily commuting which could itself cause congestion. There has been no formal quantitative attempt to assess the balance of gain in one area as against the loss in another, but it seems likely that journeys to work from place to place in the Outer Metropolitan Area are less stressful and less time consuming (distance for distance) than rush-hour travel in London.

Social balance   Just as *self-contained* means many things so does the adjective *balanced*. Some of the meanings of the word balanced have already been subsumed in the discussion of self-containment. A town would not be self-contained unless there was some balance between the needs of its population and the facilities provided for them. As already pointed out, a balance in the levels of population and employment, for example, is a necessary though not a sufficient condition for self-containment.

But most of the debate about the word balance relates to the social structures of the new towns. This topic was discussed in the Reith Committee reports in very explicit terms:

. . . The terms of reference stipulate that the new communities shall be self-contained and balanced, and we have frequently used these expressions in our reports. There is no doubt about the meaning of 'self-contained' and we have indicated how this can be brought about. There may, however, be some doubt as to the full significance of a 'balanced' community, and still more as to how that is to be achieved. So far as the issue is an economic one, balance can be attained by giving opportunity for many sorts of employment which will attract men and women up to a high income level.

Beyond that point the problem is not economic at all nor even a vaguely social one; it is, to be frank, one of class distinction. So far as these distinctions are based on income, taxation and high costs of living are reducing them. We realise also that there are some who would have us ignore their existence. But the problem remains and must be faced; if the community is to be truly balanced, so long as social classes exist, all must be represented in it. A contribution is needed from every type and class of person; the community will be the poorer if all are not there, able and willing to make it.

. . . In all existing communities there is a tendency towards segregation by income group. This is much less intractable in a town planned as a whole of which every part receives equal care in layout, architecture and amenities. This segregation is caused, especially in cities, as much by differences of social behaviour associated with differences of income as by the actual differences of income. In some respects and to some extent these differences of social behaviour are now less marked; but they have by no means disappeared and so long as they continue the tendency to segregation is understandable and it will remain. If a socially homogeneous community is to be created, a conscious and sustained policy to that end will be needed on the part of the agency itself, and of the leaders of local industry and commerce and of social activity. It will not be enough merely to attract a representative cross-section of the population, to locate skilfully the sites for houses of all classes in the various neighbourhoods, and to provide at the earliest stage suitable buildings for various amenities. These will all be essential, but more than these will be required. We believe this issue is vital to the success of these new communities; that what is achieved here may have an effect far beyond the field of its immediate application, and that there is need for much more thought and study on this subject. (Ministry of Town and Country Planning, *Final Report of the New Towns Committee*, pp 9–11)

Thus, the objective of social balance was a major one for the new towns and was largely seen in terms of class composition, both of the town as a whole and of its various neighbourhoods. Heraud, in an article in *Urban Studies* discusses the definitions of balance that came to be employed and the degree of success in achieving them attained in the new towns:

. . . What was the precise meaning of the balanced 'community' to the planners involved in the creation of the New Towns?
Generally, this has been conceived of as a reproduction of some standard or average demographic, social and industrial structure. Thus, in the development of Crawley New Town the aim was 'to achieve a similar balance to that of England and Wales in the local (New Town) population'. In social class terms, a balanced community is thus one which conforms to the class characteristics of England and Wales and most Development Corporations have used the national figures as a standard of comparison when publishing statistics on their own class distribution.

Clearly, however, two types of 'social balance' were envisaged. One would relate to the town as a whole to which, it was hoped, a socially balanced population could be attracted. However, as New Towns were to be constructed on a 'neighbourhood' basis, with services which would make each area relatively self-contained for day to day needs, even more important would be the attainment of local or neighbourhood balance. Neighbourhoods should not differ radically from one another otherwise New Towns would begin to resemble older communities in which the classes, whilst living in the same town, inhabited different areas. A Study Group of the Ministry of Town and Country Planning, reporting in 1944, recommended that 'within the neighbourhood . . . a variety of dwellings should be provided. A great deal of evidence has been submitted indicating that each neighbourhood should be "socially balanced", inhabited by families belonging to different ranges of income groups or at least not so unbalanced as to be restricted to dwellings and families of one type or income level only.'

The attainment of this aim would clearly be difficult. If the neighbourhoods were to be a broad reflection of the town as a whole then, on the basis of the 1951 England and Wales Census figures, approximately one-fifth of households would be middle class and the remainder working class. As each neighbourhood would contain approximately 2,500 dwellings, this would mean the 'dilution' of only 500 middle class families in an otherwise working class area.

The problems of social relationships which would be raised by the indiscriminate mixing of dwellings for families of different income levels were recognised by the Group. The solution suggested was the clustering of families of *similar* social class in sub-units of between 100–300 families within the neighbourhood. Thus, while neighbourhoods would be balanced in an overall sense, within this context like would be able to live with like. Already such a compromise scheme differed substantially from the aspirations of those not so closely concerned with the actual planning of communities. The Reith Committee said surprisingly little about neighbourhood balance, appearing to accept it without discussion as a planning principle.

Actual social mixing in the neighbourhoods was to be based more on the existence of certain facilities which would attract those of all classes and provide a series of 'cross cutting alliances' by which social segregation could be avoided. Such alliances, according to F. Musgrove, mitigated the worst consequence of social segregation in eighteenth-century London. Amongst the most important of these were coffee houses, taverns and parks, as well as certain Grammar Schools. In the New Towns, the most important 'cross cutting alliance' was to be the Community Centre in each neighbourhood, providing activities in which all the local population could join. As all children of primary (although not secondary) school age were to go to the same neighbourhood school, this would also be a meeting point for the classes. A neighbourhood shopping centre would also serve a similar function. However, much depended on the presence of all social classes in each neighbourhood. If neighbourhoods became one-class areas, then these facilities would lose their 'cross cutting' functions...

Table 8 Class structures of new towns, with comparisons

Social class	Crawley 1961 %	Harlow 1957 %	Hemel Hempstead 1960 %	England and Wales 1961 %	Greater London 1961 %	Dagenham 1958 %
I Professional	3·7	5·0	5·9	3·8	4·8	1
II Intermediate Professional	13·4	13·0	20·1	15·4	15·8	4
III Unskilled non-manual and skilled manual	63·6	63·0	54·6	51·1	52·2	56
IV Semi-skilled manual	13·1	}19·0	14·4	20·5	18·1	22
V Unskilled manual	6·2		5·0	9·2	9·1	17
Middle class (Classes I & II)	17·1	18·0	26·0	19·2	20·6	5
Working class (Classes III, IV and V)	82·9	82·0	74·0	80·8	79·4	95

Source: Heraud (1968)

Table 8 presents an analysis of the occupational class characteristics of three London 'ring' New Towns. Comparisons are made with the 'standard' populations of England and Wales and Greater London, together with the housing estate of Dagenham. The scale used is that of the Registrar Generals Classifications of Occupations. This ignores all but occupational criteria of stratification and fails to distinguish between manual and non-manual workers. This scale is used throughout the paper as it is the method of classification used by New Town Development Corporations in the analysis of their populations. The New Town figures represent the occupational class of heads of household of subsidised dwellings, but exclude private and new non-subsidised dwellings. The figures for the standard populations and for Dagenham represent the occupational class of all occupied and retired workers. In comparing the two sets of figures these discrepancies should be borne in mind.

The occupational class structures of the three New Towns show considerable similarities. In all cases the majority of the population are in the skilled manual/unskilled non-manual category (Social Class III), ranging from 54.6 per cent in Hemel Hempstead to 63.6 per cent in Crawley. By comparison with the 'standard' populations, such as England and Wales and Greater London, this class is over-represented in the New Towns. In the Professional (Social Class I) and Intermediate Professional (Social Class II) groups a broad similarity is shown between Crawley and Harlow and the two standard populations. In Hemel Hempstead these classes (26 per cent of the population) are proportionately considerably in excess of either England and Wales or Greater London. The three New Towns reveal almost exactly similar proportions of the semi-skilled and unskilled (approx. 19 per cent) and it is in these categories that the greatest variations from the standard populations are revealed. In England and Wales 29.7 per cent and in Greater London 27.2 per cent are in these combined categories. The low proportions of unskilled workers in the New Towns are particularly apparent. In Hemel Hempstead they make up little more than half and in Crawley about two-thirds of the national or Greater London proportions.

In general there is a striking resemblance between the New Towns and the standard populations. This is seen if, for the sake of presentation, the five occupational classes are combined into middle class (classes I and II) and working class (III, IV and V). If Hemel Hempstead is considered alone, its class structure is over-represented in favour of the middle class with over a quarter of the population in this group compared to approximately a fifth in the standard populations.

The comparison between the New Towns and an inter-war housing estate (Dagenham and Becontree) is also particularly striking. Dagenham is a largely one-class area with 95 per cent of its population in the working class. Only 1 per cent of the population are in professional employment and 4 per cent in intermediate professional jobs. In the New Towns the lowest proportion in these two groups taken together is 17.1 per cent in Crawley.

The New Towns considered here are only three out of eight in the London 'ring' of New Towns and, although widely scattered in geographical terms, may not be a representative sample. Thus only tentative conclusions can be drawn from these figures. They would seem to suggest, however, that the London New Towns have been very successful in recruiting socially balanced populations, if these are defined in terms of some national or regional average. In the words of the Social Development Officer of Hemel Hempstead 'New Towns are not settlements of any narrow range of the working class. They are occupied by a considerable range of the total income and social structure scale of the metropolitan area.' (Heraud 1968 pp 37-40)

Thomas has analysed the question of social balance in Scotland as well as England and come to similar conclusions – that the new towns have achieved a certain degree of balance but that some groups, particularly unskilled manual workers, are under-represented (Thomas 1969a and 1969b). One problem in making such assessments is that the conclusions reached will depend on what comparison groups are chosen. The use of a national average or comparison with existing towns of similar size has a certain amount of justification but the comparison as in Table 8 with housing estates which are simply parts of larger places, and therefore strictly speaking not comparable, can be considered less justified.

Comparison of the industrial structure of the new towns with the socio-economic group distributions that industries generate for the whole of

Figure 7 High income new town housing, Harlow New Town

Figure 8 Low income new town housing, Harlow New Town

Great Britain suggests that the industrial structure is a major factor in determining the class structure. Most of the new towns have a bias towards firms in the engineering industry which employ an above average proportion of professionally qualified personnel (Tables 9a and 9b). Professional workers, those in socio-economic groups 3 and 4, are over-represented in the workforces of the London new towns but not to the same extent among residents since a large proportion of this group, larger than for any other group, chooses to live outside (Table 9c).

Professional workers, as Tables 9c and 9d together demonstrate, are among the most mobile of all socio-economic groups. If the distribution of place of residence among this group in the workforce were simply due to this general characteristic of mobility then one would expect a proportion of residents working outside roughly equal to that of the workforce living outside. Table 9d shows that this is in fact not the case. Only 38 per cent of residents in employment work outside whereas 49 per cent of the workforce for this socio-economic group live outside. It is likely that there is some explanation particular to the new towns. The low proportion of houses available for purchase in the new towns compared with a national average might partly explain why many professionals live outside the new towns. This explanation should, however, apply with equal force to managers, another group which tends to have a propensity towards owner occupation. As Table 9d shows, however, managers are not much more mobile in respect of workforce than in respect of the resident working population. It is possible that London's new towns have less appeal for professionals as places in which to live. Whatever the explanation, it is worth noting that were it not for the bias in the industrial structure, London's new towns would have a deficiency of professional workers among the resident working population. Given an industrial structure less dependent on engineering, and closer to the national average, professional workers would be *under-represented* among the resident population of the London new towns rather than slightly over-represented as they are at present (see Heraud 1968 quoted above, and Thomas 1969a p 420).

There is no evidence that development corporations have in the past examined the socio-economic group structures generated by different types of industry and used this knowledge to filter the applications of prospective employers in their designated areas in order to achieve a socially balanced class structure. The result is that some groups, like professional workers, are adequately represented because of 'accidental', in the sense of being unplanned, opposing

Tables 9 a, b, c, d Illustration of the link between industrial structure and class structure of residents Source: Census of Population

Table 9a Industrial structure of selected new towns and Great Britain in 1966

| Industry | Industrial structure | | | |
| | Crawley | Glenrothes | Harlow | Great Britain |
	(percentages of total employment)			
Primary	0.3	1.3	0.2	5.5
Manufacture of engineering and electrical goods	31.8	35.6	30.0	9.0
All other manufacturing	21.2	17.9	22.9	25.8
Construction	6.3	19.5	8.7	7.8
Gas, electricity and water	0.6	0.0	0.8	1.7
Transport and communication	5.0	1.4	2.8	6.7
Distribution	10.5	6.7	10.2	13.4
Insurance, banking and finance	2.8	2.0	1.0	2.7
Professional and scientific services	10.3	9.8	14.4	10.3
Miscellaneous services	7.9	4.3	5.6	10.9
Public administration	2.8	1.4	3.2	5.8
Inadequately described	0.4	0.0	0.2	0.3

Table 9b Socio-economic groups of persons employed in
engineering compared with all persons in employment

| Socio-economic groups | Great Britain, 1966 | |
	persons employed in Industry Category VI, engineering and electrical goods %	all persons in employment %
1 Employers and managers in large establishments	3.1	2.9
2 Employers and managers in small establishments	2.0	5.0
3 Self-employed professional workers	0.0	0.5
4 Professional employees	4.7	2.8
5 Intermediate non-manual workers	2.5	6.3
6 Junior non-manual workers	18.2	21.6
7 Personal service workers	0.9	5.4
8 Foremen and supervisors—manual workers	3.7	2.5
9 Skilled manual workers	34.6	23.1
10 Semi-skilled manual workers	24.1	14.8
11 Unskilled manual workers	5.5	7.8
12 Own account workers (other than professional)	0.3	3.1
13-17 Other (farmers, agricultural workers, armed forces and indefinite)	0.3	4.2
TOTAL	99.9	100.0

Table 9c Percentage of persons working in five of London's new towns but
living outside, by socio-economic group in 1966*

Socio-economic groups	Living and working in the town %	Working in the town but living outside %	Total numbers represented
1,2 Managers	62	38	10,650
3,4 Professional workers	51	49	8,620
5,6 Other non-manual workers	74	26	47,310
9, 10, 11 Manual workers	79	21	65,700
7, 8, 12-17 Other groups, eg service industry workers	85	15	13,840
All socio-economic groups	75	25	146,120

Table 9d Percentage of employed population in five of London's
new towns working outside, by socio-economic group in 1966*

Socio-economic groups	Living and working in the town %	Living in the town but working outside %	Total numbers represented
1, 2 Managers	65	35	10,030
3, 4 Professional workers	62	38	7,080
5, 6 Other non-manual workers	82	18	42,630
9, 10, 11 Manual workers	82	18	63,240
7, 8, 12-17 Other groups eg service industry workers	83	17	14,270
All socio-economic groups	80	20	137,250

*data available from 1966 Sample Census for local authority areas only. In the cases of Crawley,
Harlow, Hemel Hempstead, Stevenage and Welwyn Garden City the local authority boundary
corresponds with the boundary of the designated area of the new town. In the case of Basildon there is
only moderate correspondence and there is no correspondence at all in the cases of Hatfield and
Bracknell with the nearest local authority areas (Hatfield rural district and Easthampstead rural district
at the 1966 Census).

influences whilst other groups, such as the unskilled, are under-represented as a direct result of the type of industry that is brought in.

The issue of social balance within neighbourhoods, an objective designed to prevent segregation within the town by class, will be considered fully in Unit 29. The main problem is that however great an effort the development corporations make to obtain a social mix within different parts of the town some will achieve a reputation for being 'better' than others. This in turn will encourage individuals to move to areas more in keeping with their own class or class aspirations and the net effect of this is likely to be increasing social segregation. In later new towns such as Milton Keynes the neighbourhood idea has been rejected and it may be that this indicates an acceptance of a certain degree of social segregation by class as inevitable.

It is probably unfair to criticize the new towns on the basis of lack of balance of other than class groups since, as the quotation given from the Final Report of the Reith Committee shows, social class was seen as the most important, if not an overriding, consideration. The relative lack of coloured immigrants in the new towns compared with, say, London may reflect positive choice on the part of new immigrants to live in reasonably close contact, at least at first, with their own cultural groups which can give them support (Rex 1968). It is a moot point whether there should be a positive effort to disperse immigrants in order to create balance. There may be perhaps unconsciously at the root of such suggestion, a fear of the concentration of a socially disadvantaged and threatening social group similar to a fear of the 'masses' of working classes concentrated in cities at the end of the last century. However, in that the new towns give the chance of improved housing, usually without a long and demoralizing wait, there should be an attempt to make sure that groups which have little contact with normal information channels are made aware of the possibilities.

Another point is that the development corporation policy of providing houses only for those with a job in the town in order to maintain a certain level of self containment automatically excludes those who have no job and are unlikely to get one for reasons of physical or mental disability. The long term unemployed and the unemployable are destined to stay where they are. In addition, in order to get a job one has to have something to offer, and in new towns with a concentration on engineering industries demanding high levels of skills this may mean that the unskilled are overall at a disadvantage. This would explain why this group seems to be under-represented in the social composition of the new towns.

Both London's and Glasgow's new towns have failed to accommodate as many members of low income groups as many planners would have liked, and it has been pointed out that they could, for example, accommodate twice their existing number of unskilled manual workers without having an unbalanced social structure. It has also been suggested that:

... The situation as it exists casts some doubt on the desirability of the goal of social balance. Carried to an extreme the pursuit of the goal might lead to development corporations making a special effort to attract employers who pay low wages – which would seem rather ludicrous. With the benefit of hindsight it appears that a satisfactory degree of social balance is achieved automatically as a result of getting a variety of different employers. As far as social policy is concerned it might be better to abandon the independent aim of social balance and instead charge the development corporations specifically with the function of ensuring that there are adequate opportunities for those without the skills necessary to earn good money. (Cresswell and Thomas 1972 p 73)

6 The terminology of persuasion

... People who come to live and work in the new town of Bracknell have a good
house in good surroundings with good amenities. The children will have grass to
play in and fresh air to breathe. But there is something else – a chance to take part in
creating a new and worthwhile community. When all is said and done, a town is made
by the people who live in it. (Statement in publicity booklet 'Bracknell' prepared by
Bracknell Development Corporation)

... I don't like to see the beauty spots being violated. My great grandfather
was here, and his father before him. We belong here, and I shouldn't like to see the
beauty being taken away. If they are going to put factories up our countryside is
going to be polluted, especially the air, and people come here specially for that. I
suffer from lung trouble, and the air at present is grand for that. Have you seen
the beauty of the place? That avenue of chestnuts, up by the school, and the parish
church? (Statement by resident of Old Stevenage, a sixty year old labourer, quoted
in Orlans 1952)

... Planned as one of the first British new towns after the war, Harlow has developed
into a prosperous community of over 70,000 people, with four clusters of neighbourhoods grouped around the new town centre, and industry located in two large and
two smaller estates. The population will rise to 90,000 or possibly even higher, but
already Harlow has become an important regional centre, and by 1967 there are some
400 local organizations reflecting an astonishing range of interests and activities.

This vigorous and exciting atmosphere is no accident. It is the result of vision and
co-operation at many levels by the Development Corporation and the Urban
District Council of Harlow and the County Council of Essex, and of the enthusiasm
and devotion of the many Harlow people who give their time to the voluntary
organizations. (Statement in publicity booklet 'Living in Harlow' prepared by
Harlow Development Corporation)

... When a cabinet member speaks of 'avoiding chaos', 'organic balance', 'creative
possibilities', 'building poems', 'communities of tomorrow' and the like, he is reading
burnished but rather empty rhetoric taken by his speech writer from current exponents
of a long tradition of architectural and utopian writers. Further, certain code words
are commonly used. For instance, one of the most frequent reasons for wanting
new towns is that they will be 'planned' (a word used in urban matters as a term of

praise acceptable to both the political left and right). But the fact *per se* that something is to be planned is of interest only to the professionals who get the work and also to later chroniclers. To others, such planning is an input and the question is one of output: what does such planning do to what the new town will do? In this particular case, 'planning' stands for certain land use and circulation features, lower costs through reduction of uncertainty in infra-structure investment, and so forth. Some other code words are 'balanced', 'exciting', 'variety', 'living environment', 'choice' and 'human scale'. (Statement in an article by William Alonso, Professor of Regional Planning at the University of California, Berkeley, Alonso 1970)

This selection of extracts is intended to illustrate some of the different views about the new towns and the ways in which these are put forward by different individuals and groups. The last extract quoted, by Professor Alonso, makes an important point that certain words appear as tokens, code words, which are almost drained of meaning because of the exaggerated and partisan way in which they are used. Some of these words also represent a conflict in meaning by groups, usually proponents or opponents of the new towns, who wish to put forward their particular versions of reality. In this section there will be an examination of the use of such key words in attempts to persuade others of the truth of a particular view. The following section on 'indirect control' will consider how the development corporations set about their aims of bringing employment and population to the new towns. Attempts at persuading the public, or more specifically prospective inhabitants, will of course feature among these.

In the preceding section of this unit the main objective was to discuss the extent to which new towns have achieved objectives which were specified for them. The point, which will have become apparent from the analysis is that all these objectives relate to ways in which it is thought that people should live. The taking of population from large cities (described as 'excess' or 'overspill' population) is simultaneously an attempt to change these cities by reducing overall population density in the direction of being, if anything, less city-like and to set up relatively smaller settlements which can be planned on a more comprehensible scale. The objective of self-containment is linked with the feeling that places should have an identity, that if more people do more things in a place they will 'belong' to it more strongly through their actions and their feelings. The objective of social balance is linked with the hope that the mixing of different class groups will promote greater interaction and understanding between them. It is linked with the more general idea that all sectional groups in a place should mix together, perhaps on the basis of regarding the strength, frequency and inclusiveness of interactions as a measure of 'success'.

To put it simply, the proponents of new towns believe that people are happier living in new towns than in alternative types of place, ranging from exurban villages to big cities. The sort of places that people are happy living in – that are in these terms 'successful' – are described as 'communities', a word which has associated with it a variety of meanings as you will know from reading Dennis' article (in Pahl 1968). Elements such as the provision of local facilities for local group activities, the existence of common interests and understandings and the strength and frequency of interaction can all form part of the definition of community. Thus it is that goals such as social balance and self-containment which relate to a number of the supposedly positive elements of social life are being promoted in order to attain a much vaguer and more embracing goal, the achievement of the creation of a 'community'. There is, therefore, in much of the discussion of goals such as self-containment an underlying debate, an underlying argument that the new towns are (or are not) 'communities'.

The word itself features strongly in the literature produced by planners, whether in the Reith reports which had, according to their terms of reference, the objective of setting out a framework for creating new towns as 'self-contained and balanced communities for work and living', or in publicity material produced by development corporations or in the master plans of new towns. If you look in the Reith reports or in any of these other sources you will have to look hard to find a definition of the word 'community'. For a word which can have a number of meanings and which is often used, in practice it is strangely little defined.

One reason for the general vagueness may be that it is easy to assume that the set of meanings one has is shared by the listener or reader, particularly with a concept which is widely used. It may be assumed that the meaning is self-evident though as was noted above, following the argument produced by Dennis, there can be a multitude of meanings. Failure to define the term and its ambiguous or confusing usage may often be the result of simple oversight. This in itself causes problems when any attempt is made to analyse the degree of attainment of goals or other appraisals of the situation.

A further dimension is added to the problem when it is recognized that the word 'community' has in fact two main *types* of meaning. One is as a straight-forward description of a place where people live: in this sense it is more or less synonymous with the words 'place' or 'settlement'. The other type is that which has already been described: meanings which relate to the adjudged 'successful' state of a number of people living in the same place, with the degree of success being seen in frequency, strength or inclusiveness of interactions and the existence of local institutions. As Alonso (1970) pointed out, in this sense the word indicates *approval* by whatever criteria one chooses to adopt of a number of people living in a place. The use of the word 'community' alternately in two different senses, or in both senses at the same time, gives an advantage in rhetoric to anyone making out a particular case.

A real difficulty in trying to cope with the arguments of different interest groups lies in the fact that it is difficult to avoid using words in an ordinary sense which also have a special meaning. Thus a development corporation will claim to be 'building a community' and a Residents' Protection Association in the same area may claim that the development corporation is 'destroying an established community'.

The truth is that a new settlement will be built and an established settlement will be altered. Whether, and to what degree, either of these are or were communities in the second general sense of the term is a matter open to analysis and debate. If, in communicating with either of these organizations, one is forced into adopting the special usages of terms that they employ in their particular description of social life in the area, their version of reality, will *de facto* have been accepted.

The word 'community' is thus often used in the context of arguments which amount to propaganda. It is one of a number of key words which themselves embody preferred versions of reality. Because it has an everyday, ordinary usage from which it would be difficult to be dislodged, it is very effective. This is because, as we have argued, shifts in meaning from a purely descriptive usage to an affective usage can occur within an argument and be tantamount to a claim which will go unchallenged, disguised as it is in an apparent uniformity in the use of terms. Those who use the word, call forth support in themselves, their supporters who might be members of the group which is defined as a 'community' and in any apparently disinterested audience. In transactions between groups which threaten each other, or are striving to achieve an identity, it is a vital emotive word. It is used frequently in the descriptions by planners of their actions and of groups defending their interests from planners, for example the local protection societies for existing places that often arise when the creation of a new town is threatened. Since the word is used as a claim both for support and for a particular state of being it is not just a version of reality but, in a condensed form, a sociological charter.

An analysis of the situation may reveal that far from being solidary, a 'community' even under threat can reveal basic differences. Orlans (1952) noted that in Stevenage the core of the Residents' Protection Association were formed by middle class outsiders who had come to the village to escape from town life in addition to local people with their roots in the area.

. . . The New Town was regarded by many influential sources as part of the urban onslaught upon rural life which must be resisted. Many had themselves moved from London to escape the city; now it was thrust upon them. 'I came here to be out of the dirt and din', said a business man who continued to commute to work in London. 'Now look what's happening. I'm going to be right in the middle of it.' Like him, many of the most active leaders of the Residents' Protection Association were not natives but London business men. 'It wasn't the natives of Stevenage who made the most noise over the new town,' said one (native) informant. They were joined, of course, and stoutly supported by natives, who like a sixty year old labourer considered it sacrilege to disturb scenes familiar since childhood . . . (Orlans 1952 p 139)

Other groups may find that they have divided loyalties, particularly those who stand to gain or lose in a financial sense fairly heavily. Local shopkeepers may feel that the influx of population will give an enormous boost to trade. On the other hand if they are excluded from new shopping developments they may find that they are in a backwater, perhaps worse off than they were before. Farmers, whether tenants or owners, have an interest in securing as much compensation as possible. While at the beginning they may devote all their energies to stopping the proposed new town, when the tide has turned irrevocably against them they will want to devote all their energies to secure adequate compensation. This conflict of interest was demonstrated at the public enquiry into the designation of Milton Keynes New City where farmers' representatives made their objection in the strongest terms on the grounds that valuable agricultural land would be taken up, but in the same breath asked, if it was to be taken up, for favourable compensation terms.

. . . On Wednesday, [6 July 1966] the objections heard were mainly those of organized agriculture, the attack being led by Mr Neville Wallace who appeared for both the National Farmers Union Steering Committee and the National Union of Agricultural Workers . . .
'The same concern at these new town proposals is felt by farm workers as it is by the farmers,' he said.
'The fact that these two principal sections of the agricultural industry, who often appear on opposite sides of the table, have joined forces is proof, not only of the unity of the agricultural case, but of the strength of opinion and sincerity of all concerned in the industry in believing the designation order before us to be disastrous.'
'The huge size of this project is something that the minds of most of us cannot comprehend and therefore makes it all the more difficult to oppose,' he said.
His submission, he said, fell under four heads.
First, they said that the information on which the Ministry relied was often, so far as agriculture was concerned, either inaccurate or incomplete, with the result that its deductions were not valid.

Secondly, they said that the concept of a new town in the light of modern national needs and national agriculture was 'out-dated and obsolete' and that it should be discarded – especially when the concept was taken to the lengths which characterized the present proposal.

Thirdly they said that the development which they admitted must come to the area, must also involve less disruption of agriculture in its size and effect.

Fourthly, they said that farmers and farm workers should not be expected to make a greater sacrifice in the interests of development than was required by other sections of industry – and that if they had to be sacrificed, then compensation should be realistic and business-like. (Bletchley District Gazette 1966)

The defence of 'community' may then be weakened by sectional interests. In the case of Milton Keynes there were a number of different villages and towns in the designated area which acted against the proposed new city, but less effectively than if they had combined as a single threatened entity. One of the existing towns, Bletchley, was already subject to an overspill agreement with the Greater London Council, and so largely populated by newcomers. Here the local council supported the new scheme. Presumably they felt that they had much to gain in the way of increased facilities for their greatly expanded population and little to lose at this stage in the ways of rural atmosphere.

Returning to the planners' version of reality, in the face of local opposition their actions are likely to be justified by the argument that they are serving the needs of the 'community' *outside* the local area. In the case of London's new towns the community cited outside is likely to be London itself. Since the views of this 'community' cannot be suddenly canvassed the development corporations are left as spokesmen with a contention which though it cannot be justified simply and easily, is also especially difficult to deny. Once having started to build the new town itself a development corporation can refer to the 'community' that it feels it is beginning to create.

There are a number of other everyday words which can come to act as concentrated propaganda, as sociological charters, besides the word 'community', though this of course is crucial in the context of new towns. The word 'slum', for example, has strong emotional overtones and is often used to describe areas in bad housing condition. The 1954 Housing Act lists a number of criteria by which a dwelling can be described as 'unfit' but does not itself use the word 'slum'. It is probably more effective for a group making out a case of neglect by a local authority or for a local authority that wishes to clear an area to describe the area as a 'slum' rather than use the more neutral term 'unfit' (see also Unit 28).

Another key word, or code word in Alonso's terms, is 'home'. Builders manifestly provide houses yet they will claim on their advertisements to be building 'homes'. A home, of course, implies more than simply a house; it implies occupation by a family or other group and, unless the word is qualified, it implies relatively successful living together. The word tends to trigger a whole set of associations in an individual which relate to his own background. The builder claims to be providing a home, which *in fact* will have to be provided by the buyer, in order, perhaps by claiming more, to be able to ask for a higher price. There is possibly also an implication that in a superior environment things just can't fail to work. Development corporations also, in literature produced by public relations staff or consultants, claim to be providing homes rather than houses. It is part of the dream of 'community' which they are selling.

Words which are used as charters to persuade, convince, engender support, provoke a response or allay criticism are part of the means by which individuals or institutions attempt to exert control over each other. They may not be used with specific, controlled and conscious intent (as perhaps some propaganda speeches are designed, say, to demoralize an enemy's civilian population) but they are used with a general intention and in ways in which individuals naturally and artfully try to influence each other.

The next section of this unit deals with some of the methods by which development corporations ensure that their towns are filled with people and industry and do not become ghost towns from the start. Persuasion that the venture is, or will be, a success and that a 'community' is being generated provides part of the means by which people and firms will be persuaded to come. It is much the same process as that advocated by Marshall as long ago as 1884 (see quote in Section 2). It is not however by itself enough to ensure that the operation of attracting people will succeed and other means of indirect control will need to be employed.

7 Strategic interaction and indirect control

Under the New Towns and Town Development Acts development corporations and local authorities have the powers to purchase compulsorily buildings and land within the designated areas of their towns. They also have the power to develop land so acquired for housing, industry, roads and other essential services. They have no powers under these Acts, or through any other legislation, to compel individuals and firms to move to the new towns. To increase the chances of success for these and other related goals, resort has had to be made to more indirect methods of control. These have chiefly consisted of incentives which tend to structure the environment of choices presented to individuals and organizations but do not compel them to act in any particular way. A successful outcome will occur providing sufficient individuals are influenced to act in a way required to produce some desired overall effect.

In addition to the major aim of attracting enough people and sufficient employers to get a town off the ground most development corporations have taken seriously the objectives of social balance and self-containment which were given special emphasis in the Reith reports. The attraction of roughly equal volumes of population and employment will allow for the achievement of self-containment in terms of journeys to work but, as was noted in Section 5, this will not guarantee success. Some other control will have to be operated to prevent possible large inward and outward commuting flows. Social balance is very difficult to guarantee. In respect of social class, a framework for social balance can be provided by controlling the influx of employers such that the industrial structure will allow for a balanced class structure. Development corporations do not seem to have made any systematic attempt to do this (see Section 5) and the resulting socio-economic group structure seems to have just 'happened' as a result of a general preference for clean light engineering industries rather than having been planned.

There have of course been a variety of individual objectives for different new towns. For the group of new towns which have been defined in this unit as satellite new towns one overall objective was to take overspill population from the parent cities. This again was an objective spelt out in the Reith reports. The means used to achieve this and the other objectives so far listed will be discussed below.

In order simply to get people and jobs, development corporations attempt through means such as advertisement campaigns, press releases and contacts with employers and 'exporting' local authorities to present as favourable an image of themselves as possible. People and firms are more likely, it is felt, to move to a place if they feel that it is a success and can offer them more than their present environment. A similar process of self-presentation to that employed by the development corporations is, of course, employed by any organization that has something to sell or, rather, as in this case, something that it *must* sell.

The special feature of the new towns situation from a marketing point of view is the resistance encountered in the form of local protection associations, national countryside and farming associations and other individuals and groups opposed to the new towns. In addition to 'normal' persuasion and advertising, development corporations are often involved in a conflict which centres around a disputed definition of the situation through the use of key words such as 'community'. Such words provide a focus for conflict because of the special meanings which attach to them in addition to their ostensible, 'ordinary' meanings. This is the particular aspect of the new town idea that was discussed in the previous section.

To attract people in sufficient numbers and under appropriate conditions to fulfil other objectives such as self-containment, the facility offered by development corporations with the greatest potential power of attraction was housing. The conditions under which this was offered could be used as a way of indirectly controlling the characteristics of the incoming population. Thus, in most of the satellite new towns, housing was normally offered only to those who had obtained a job in the town and who came from the parent city. A further condition was that priority was usually given to those considered to be in greatest housing need. To some extent this latter condition was offset by the need to ensure that incomers would be 'good tenants' and by the hurdle that the applicant had to overcome of obtaining a job in the town.

The first of the controls described in the previous paragraph of offering housing only to those with a job in this town has, at least for the London new towns, tended to make for an initial situation of relative self-containment. As was described in Section 5 the conditions, for the successful operation of this control for example, monopoly of housing, are being eroded with the passage of time. The erosion of control in this area will be further accelerated by the government decision in 1970 to begin to sell houses in the new towns to bring the level of owner occupation up to the national average of fifty per cent of households.

The second control of giving priority to housing applicants from the parent city has operated to ensure that the majority of newcomers come as intended overspill population. By 1968, 63 per cent of tenancies for the eight London new towns had been let to Londoners (Roderick 1971). That the figure is not much higher is mainly due to limitations on the control itself. For large firms with many branches in different parts of the country exception has to be made for transfer of staff between branches. Exception also had to be made for public servants transferred to work in a new town, such as local government employees, civil servants and hospital staff. Employers also found it essential to recruit key workers and specialist workers from as wide an area as possible. In practice this often meant any job which required special qualifications and for which there was strong competition. Another point is that in recent years many tenancies have been allocated (or houses sold) to local people who have grown up in the town, ie 'second generation immigrants', and who thus compete with incomers for available housing. In the early years of development

Figure 10 The industrial selection scheme

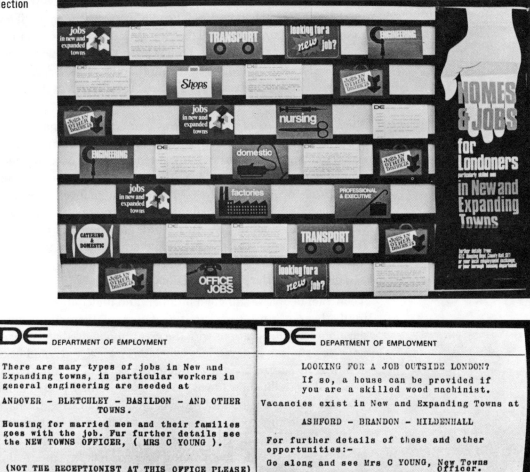

such a problem is usually absent and a greater proportion of houses can at this time be allocated to incomers from the parent city.

In London and other cities an Industrial Selection Scheme exists for those prepared to move out to a new or expanding town. This operates through local authorities asking individuals on their housing waiting lists, or who are considered to be in housing need, whether they would be prepared to move to a new town. The names of those who respond positively go on to a register together with details of their occupation and qualifications. In London this list is kept by the Greater London Council. When vacancies occur in a new or expanded town that cannot be filled locally, details of these are passed on to the parent city authority by the Department of Employment. The city authority then nominates candidates who are subsequently interviewed by officials at their local employment exchanges. Details of candidates considered suitable are then passed on to the employer who will interview from among these. Individuals offered employment in this way then become eligible for rented new town housing.

The Industrial Selection Schemes are lengthy and impersonal and many individuals bypass this scheme by applying directly for jobs in the new towns which they hear about through personal contacts. Of these, a number are still motivated by the desire to obtain housing although they may not be on the housing lists for various reasons. These are likely to include the fact that there is often a two or three year wait from registration before an offer of a council house is made. In these circumstances many will not have bothered to register at all. In the case of the London new towns, for example, only about ten per cent of migrants go through the Industrial Selection Scheme. But in the case of the expanded towns the indirect controls operated by the local authorities concerned are more effective and seventy to seventy-five per cent of those moving to local authority housing in the town go through the Industrial Selection Scheme.

The housing situation in cities like London and Glasgow, as well as being a factor that led to the decision to create satellite new towns, is a factor that operates in favour of the objectives of development corporations which are able to offer housing either immediately or after a relatively short wait. The concentration on building satellite new towns and clearing in cities rather than rebuilding at the same or higher densities does therefore also operate as a form of indirect control. The individual on a housing list who has been contacted and offered the possibility of a house in a new town can choose to reject the offer and ignore the pressures which are acting cumulatively on him to move. He cannot, however, exist outside of these pressures. His environment of choices has been structured for him, both by agencies such as the development corporations and through the operation of the housing market.

It must not be thought that the choices presented by virtue of government sponsored planning are the only possible alternatives that could have been offered. For those who were in housing need after the Second World War in cities like London there was an overwhelming desire for better housing coupled with a natural desire to stay in London if at all possible, as a government conducted social survey in North London showed at the time (Hutchinson 1947). The planners chose to attempt to satisfy the former desire but ignore the latter, either because they thought it too expensive or too difficult to carry through the programme needed to redevelop and provide adequate housing in cities, or because they were already committed to the garden city idea.

Development corporations or local authorities in the case of the expanded towns will tend to assess the success of the various strategies involved in numerical terms. It does not matter to them if particular individuals ignore incentives offered, providing enough individuals are influenced to achieve an overall effect. Again, providing overall objectives are achieved, it does not matter if particular individuals get round the rules in order to achieve their own objectives though, of course, this could have undesirable effects such as producing bad publicity.

This brings the argument to another point which is that, although individuals are often depicted as passive clients, as passive recipients of the end products of action taken on their behalf, this is not always the case. Very often individuals are pursuing their own strategies which may or may not be in accordance with the aims of the development corporations. The result in these instances can be a process of strategic interaction, defined by Goffman as follows:

... Two or more parties must find themselves in a well-structured situation of mutual impingement where each party must make a move and where every possible move carries fateful implications for all of the parties. In this situation, each player must influence his own decision by his knowing that the other players are likely to dope out his decision in advance, and may even appreciate that he knows this is likely. Courses of action or moves will then be made in the light of one's thoughts about the others' thoughts about oneself. An exchange of moves made on the basis of this kind of orientation to self and others can be called strategic interaction. (Goffman 1970 pp 100-1)

Possibly few interactions between individuals and institutions are played out in the hard and calculated fashion suggested by Goffman's game analogy. There are instances, however, where individuals take advantage of the strategies which are operated by development corporations trying to put into effect various indirect controls. An individual will, for example, attempt to obtain employment in a new town in order to get a house but without any intention of keeping the job, and sometimes with the specific intention of leaving the job as soon as he has a house. Cases of this sort have come to light incidentally in a survey recently conducted in Stevenage by the Open University New Towns Study Unit. In these cases part of the process of strategic interaction is involved with the individual's presentation of himself as a suitable employee to employer and as a suitable resident to the development corporation, and the employer's and development corporation's efforts to 'dope out' the applicant's real intentions. That the development corporations are aware of this sort of strategy employed by individuals is shown by a comment of one housing manager 'It means that any Tom, Dick or Harry can put his name down for a house. Some only take a job in the new town in order to get a house' (quoted in Thomas 1969a p 427).

It may not be particularly crucial to the development corporations if a few individuals manage to 'beat the system'. Such actions if succesful are however likely to discredit the development corporations by making them appear foolish, certainly less competent and efficient than they might like to appear, and may also act as an example to others. For these reasons the development corporations are likely to take seriously their interactions with prospective residents.

Strategic interactions are also likely to take place between employers and the development corporations who will have overlapping but not coincident objectives. Employers will want on the whole to operate free from restrictions whilst the new town planners will want to impose restrictions sufficient to achieve their aims. This may, for example, result in development corporations in the satellite new towns allowing a wide latitude for the definition of 'key workers', who need not be recruited from London through the usual channels, in order to get the employers to co-operate with the prescribed methods of recruiting for the rest of the workforce.

A whole range of largely undocumented interactions must occur between development corporations that tend to have a monopoly of resources and newly constituted local authorities in the new town areas. The latter will of course want to exercise as much control as possible whilst the development corporations, having carried through a plan from its early stages, may resent suggested alterations by local councils which are nevertheless acting as the elected representatives of the now existing local urban population.

It must finally be made clear that to describe a process of strategic interaction is not to condemn any party involved. Neither individuals nor institutions are totally free from guile. In competitive situations the guileless individual will be at an enormous disadvantage. Thus individuals and institutions employ strategies to achieve their ends. For individuals the objective may be a house to rent, a mortgage or a better job, for development corporations the attraction of people and employers of the appropriate kinds and numbers. Furthermore, planners, as well as carrying out socially approved goals, are also engaged in playing out their utopian dreams. It is the planners' conception of reality which has sway, at least as a blueprint, and their clients, who may all along have wanted something else, who have to fit in as best they can.

Figure 11 The vanishing point of landlords rent Source: Howard (1898)

8 Do new towns pay?

The economic theory underlying Ebenezer Howard's new towns proposals has two major elements. First that new towns should provide an escape from the high level of property rents in major cities. Secondly that increases in the value of property in the new town should accrue in some way to the inhabitants of the new town itself. The final question considered in this unit is the validity of this theory, particularly in the light of the British new towns experience.

One line of criticism of Howard's theory is that it is concerned predominantly with a redistribution of income and wealth – away from the landlord towards those who do not own property and therefore have to pay rent for the right to occupy a dwelling. Howard in fact went further and suggested that ultimately the surplus revenue of the new town municipalities should be used for old age pensions (see Figure 11). The dominance of this redistribution element in the economic theory suggests that new towns may not be the only way of achieving the goal. Why should not a more equitable distribution of income and wealth between tenant and property owner be achieved in quite different ways? You will remember from Unit 14, for example, that Henry George advocated tax on land values to achieve the same kind of goal. If measures of this kind could be effective why bother with all the complex machinery of planning new towns including persuasion, propaganda and the operation of indirect controls? Why bother to plan *towns* in order to achieve *social* goals?

One answer which can be given to this line of criticism is simply that there is no evidence that other means of achieving this desired redistribution away from the landlord and towards the tenant are effective. Henry George's ideas for heavy taxation of land values have not been put into practice. Over the past twenty years land and property values in nearly every country of the world have inflated at a very rapid rate. There appears to have been a steady redistribution of income and wealth in the reverse direction to that advocated by Howard. Inflation benefits property owners not tenants. The major factors which have mitigated this trend have been rent control and the growth of owner occupation. Rent control can keep rent increases in line with, or below, the inflationary trends. The growth of owner occupation has favoured a redistribution of wealth towards a large minority, if not a majority, of the population, but increasingly disadvantages those who are not property owners.

A quite different line of criticism is that the new towns have not in fact achieved a redistribution on the lines advocated by Howard. It can be pointed out that while wages in the new town tend to be slightly lower than in the parent city, both rents and food prices tend to be higher. The migrant to the new town usually betters himself substantially with regard to his housing and the purely physical aspects of his environment but, in financial terms, he is often worse off than he was in the parent city. It has been estimated, for example, that more than two-thirds of registrants on London's Industrial Selection Scheme would be worse off in terms of earnings minus rent if they moved to a new town (Gee 1972 p 28). But though it seems likely that many people do move to new towns in spite of the higher cost of living there, no systematic studies have been made comparing the budgets of new town and parent city households.

Underlying this line of criticism is the suggestion that it is unrealistic or utopian to suppose that any practical means can be found whereby the value of property in the new town accrues to the benefit of those inhabitants who rent their dwellings. This suggestion is difficult to refute on the basis of the British new towns experience.

Howard recognized that new town building would not be financially profitable in the early years and this recognition is fully borne out in the history of the new towns. Neither Letchworth nor Welwyn Garden City were financially successful in the early stages. The only redistribution of income and wealth which did occur in association with these developments was from the pockets of the philanthropists who put money into the First Garden City Company and Welwyn Garden City Ltd, without for many years receiving any dividend (Purdom 1949).

The financial position of towns developed under the New Towns Acts is not dissimilar. In the case of Milton Keynes new city designated in 1967, for example, the Development Corporation had by 1972 spent nearly £20 million on capital expenditure. A third of this was for 9,000 acres of land, and much of the rest was for expenditure on items like roads, sewers and the costs of setting up the corporation to plan and administer development. The Development Corporation received only a little over £170,000 in rent. Interest payments on capital borrowed by the Development Corporation amounted to just over £1 million in the year ending 31 March 1972 and the financial deficit was only a little under £900,000.

As the new town grows, however, both the volume and level of rents increase because of the growth of the town. Most of the new towns designated in the early postwar years are now financially viable and some of them make substantial profits. One of the most successful in financial terms is Harlow New Town in Essex. As you can see from Table 10, Harlow in the financial year ending 31 March 1971 earned a surplus of £840,000.

Most of the income received by Harlow Development Corporation in this financial year comprised housing rents amounting to more than £3 million. Even after outgoings like estate management, repairs, and maintenance are subtracted, the earnings from housing rents were more than £2 million. On industrial and commercial property outgoings were relatively small and earnings amounted to £1.5 million. The total of property rents less outgoings of £3.5 million was £0.5 million greater than interest payments.

Table 10 General revenue account for Harlow Development Corporation for year ending 31 March 1971

Expenditure:		Thousand £'s
Interest payable to the Secretary of State for the Environment		3,154
Provision for depreciation		315
Corporation Tax		150
Other expenditure		137
Balance being surplus for the year carried to Balance Sheet		841
Total		**4,597**
Income:		
Housing rents etc.	3,184	
Less outgoings	1,018	
Net Rents		2,166
Industrial rents	939	
Less outgoings	12	
Net Rents		927
Commercial and other rents	546	
Less outgoings	86	
Net Rents		460
Housing Subsidy		710
Other income		334
Total		**4,597**

Source: Reports of the Development Corporations, 31 March 1971, London, HMSO

A number of other major items like housing subsidies received from the Department of the Environment, corporation tax, depreciation and other income enter into the general revenue account. It might be argued that these accounts are distorted by the inclusion of housing subsidies – although these are paid by the government on the same basis as for other local authorities, and might be considered as matching the various fiscal advantages, such as tax relief on mortgage interest payments, enjoyed by owner occupiers. It might equally be argued that it is ridiculous to include corporation tax in the accounts of a public body because it merely represents a transfer of money from one central government account to another. But whatever the justification for the inclusion or exclusion of any particular item, it is clear that Harlow Development Corporation had by 1971 as far as its financial matters are concerned emerged firmly into the black, and had already begun to pay back to the government a substantial amount of the loans needed to finance construction of the town.

The financial benefits of Harlow New Town do not however accrue to its inhabitants. The profits earned go back to the Exchequer. The local authority – at the time of writing Harlow Urban District – has no say in how these monies are spent.

As far as the income and wealth redistribution functions of new towns are concerned the central issue is the control of property rights. You will remember from Section 2 that Howard advocated a trust which would be financially responsible to the local council. You will remember from Section 4 that although it was intended in the 1946 Act that the development corporation assets should be handed to local councils, the 1959 Act removed this provision on the grounds that it is 'unwise to mix estate management with politics'.

As much as any other issue, the new towns raise the question of what is the appropriate *level* of public ownership and decision making. The British experience of building new towns under development corporations has not provided any evidence one way or the other as to the soundness of these aspects of Howard's ideas. It may be that the experience of the expanded towns will provide relevant evidence. But so far no studies of their development have covered this topic.

In the future, however, it seems likely that both new and expanded towns will increasingly be influenced by national housing policies. Policies currently being followed are contrary to Howard's ideas because they reduce the control which can be exercised by local authorities. Under the 1972 Housing Finance Act the level of rents is fixed by government appointed rent officers and government appointed rent scrutiny boards. It seems likely that the influence of local authorities on these bodies will be even less than any influence they might have on development corporations. In the case of the expanded towns the effect of the 1972 Housing Finance Act appears to be that any financial surpluses earned through the renting of houses will be returned to the central government just as they are in the case of the new towns with development corporations.

One of the objectives of the 1972 Housing Finance Act is to encourage the growth of owner occupation. In the case of the new towns, as already mentioned in Section 3, this policy is reinforced by other measures. The development corporations are instructed to move towards a position corresponding to the national average of fifty per cent of dwellings in owner occupation and fifty per cent rented. This is very different from the position which obtained in the new towns up to the late 1960s at which time eighty per cent of dwellings were still rented. This policy is pursued both by increasing production of houses for sale and by encouraging sales to existing tenants through price reductions of twenty per cent. As a result of these policies it seems likely that levels of owner occupation in the new towns will increase dramatically over the next few years.

A high level of owner occupation might in some ways seem consistent with the spirit of Howard's ideas. The new town resident as owner occupier does benefit from the increase in property values associated with new town growth. This benefit is not direct: the market value of a house may increase from £5,000 to £15,000, but the house is still the same house and the occupier realizes no financial gain for as long as he remains the owner occupier. Even if he sells the house the financial gain is not of much practical value if he is obliged to pay about the same amount for a similar house in another locality. But the benefit can take tangible form if an owner occupier sells his house to acquire another house which is cheaper or better suited to his needs, and the owner occupier does possess a financial asset which can be used through an assurance arrangement to provide income on retirement or which can be passed on to his heirs.

Howard's scheme did not anticipate the conditions of an affluent society. His idea was that the benefits of increases in new town property values should go to the local council. Such an arrangement would give the opportunity for the financial benefits to be distributed in whatever way was thought appropriate by the local council. This might involve keeping rents and rates at a low level which would benefit tenants as well as owner occupiers. It might involve, as indicated in Figure 11, the provision of pensions for all retired inhabitants of the town and not just those who could arrange private assurance schemes. The short answer to the question posed in the title of this section is that although new towns do pay as they mature, the principal beneficiaries are not those the new town idealists originally had in mind.

Self-assessment questions

SAQ 1   Make a list of the advantages of the 'Town-Country Magnet' as shown in Figure 3 stating in each case whether you think the British new towns have actually achieved each item on the list.

SAQ 2   The unit stated in Section 2 that Herbert Spencer in his book *Social Statics* advocated that land should be held by society as a whole and that all rents should be paid to public officials. What is the difference between this view and those of Henry George described in Unit 14?

SAQ 3   Howard stated that Spencer changed his mind on the policy described in SAQ2 partly because he realized he was advocating nationalization of land. Do you think Howard's interpretation is correct?

SAQ 4   In what ways could it be said that the new towns are nationalized?

SAQ 5   Distinguish three meanings of the word 'self-contained' as used in association with Britain's new towns.

SAQ 6   Distinguish four meanings of the word 'balanced' as used in association with Britain's new towns.

SAQ 7   Define in the form of an equation the index of commuting independence.

SAQ 8   Calculate indexes of commuting independence for central London and for Greater London from the data given in Tables 5 and 7 in Unit 23, Section 7.

SAQ 9   A town has a job ratio of 120. What is the maximum value that the index of commuting independence can have?

SAQ 10   A town has a balance in respect of the levels of employment and population and yet has a low index of commuting independence – less than 0.5. Explain.

SAQ 11   Using the data given in Tables 9c and 9d calculate for the socio-economic groups *Managers* and *Manual workers*:
a   the average job ratio
b   the average index of commuting independence

SAQ 12   What are the main problems which new towns face in attempting to accommodate members of low income groups?

SAQ 13   The term *sociological charter* is used in Section 6 but no explicit definition is given. Write down a definition of this term.

SAQ 14 A council report on a proposed overspill scheme says that 'the community is likely to respond positively to the proposal'. In what way exactly does this statement incorporate *a preferred version of reality*?

SAQ 15 No definition of the term *indirect controls* used in Section 7 is given in the unit. Which of the following would you say are defining characteristics of *indirect controls*?
a Power is exercised to preclude individual choice.
b Power is not exercised to preclude individual choice.
c Rules are applied without regard to the end result.
d A net end result is being aimed at.
e The environment of individual choice is structured.
f The aim is to prevent individuals being aware of the nature of the controls operated.

SAQ 16 In what ways have Howard's ideas, and those of the 1946 New Towns Committee become less relevant because of widespread changes in land and property ownership?

SAQ 17 At the end of the unit it is stated that the principal beneficiaries from the British new towns have not been those the idealists originally had in mind. Who have been the principal beneficiaries? And who has lost out?

A guide to further reading

As mentioned in the introduction there is scarcely any material in any of the set books which is directly relevant to the objectives of this unit. The only exception is in Blumenfeld, H. (1971) *The Modern Metropolis*, which includes a few prescient remarks on new towns in the essay entitled 'Alternative Solutions for Metropolitan Development'. The best guide to further reading is contained in the references given in the text of the unit.

In order to learn more about the origins and main features of the new town idea in accordance with objective 1 you could well look at the relevant chapters of Ashworth (1954), any available edition of Ebenezer Howard's book, and the Reports of the Committee on New Towns (The Reith Reports). On the definition of new towns there does not appear to be any particularly recommendable publication other than Eichler and Kaplan (1967) and Unit 24. Neither of these studies addresses itself directly to objective 2, but they do contain a good deal of background material, which taken in conjunction with this unit is very relevant.

Objectives 2, 3 and 4 are probably covered in as much detail in this unit as in other publications. The difficulties of evaluating Britain's new towns in accordance with objective 6 have already been mentioned. Almost any publication on the new towns is relevant but the criteria which can be used in evaluation are so various that no single study can by itself be regarded as particularly recommendable. Of the publications mentioned in the text Thomas (1969a and 1969b) focuses on an evaluation in accordance with the stated aims of the development corporations. That by Schaffer (1972) is a rather uncritical study but is the best overall account of the practical problems and the way in which they were tackled by the development corporations. The book by Purdom (1949) is a comprehensive account of the development of Letchworth and the early history of Welwyn Garden City but much is of relevance to later developments under the New Town Acts.

The main studies not mentioned in the text are:

OSBORN, F. J. and WHITTOCK, A. (1969) *The New Towns – The Answer to Megalopolis*, Leonard Hill, which is particularly strong on urban design factors.

MERLIN, P. (1971) *New Towns*, Methuen, which aims to compare the new towns experience of a number of countries including the Netherlands, France, Scandinavia, Poland and Hungary as well as Britain.

For a striking contrast both in approach and subject matter there are sociological studies of two of the US Levittowns mentioned in Section 3:

DOBRINER, W. M. (1963) *Class in Suburbia*, Prentice-Hall.

GANS, H. (1967) *The Levittowners – Anatomy of suburbia: The birth of society and politics in an American town*, Allen Lane, The Penguin Press.

Answers to SAQs

Answer SAQ 1

Advantage	*Achievement*
Beauty of nature	Doubtful. New towns too urban in character, but see answer to 'fields and parks. . .'
Social opportunity	Yes, in the sense that new towns provide the opportunity for more social interaction than rural areas.
Fields and parks of easy access	Fields no. But one of the characteristic features of new towns is a generous provision of parks and public open space.
Low rents	Probably low relative to London but not relative to other cities.
High wages	Not compared with cities.
Low rates	No.
Plenty to do	Yes as far as employment is concerned, but only in years of maturity as far as many other facilities are concerned.
Low prices	No
No sweating	Sweated labour is hopefully rare in Britain nowadays.
Field for enterprise	New town manufacturing industries seem to be buoyant. But there seems to be difficulty for very small enterprises, such as one-man businesses, in finding suitable premises, etc.
Flow of capital	Yes, but from government or exporting authority.
Pure air and water	Yes. New town industries not generally polluting.
Good drainage	Yes
Bright homes and gardens	Yes
No smoke	Yes
No slums	Yes, but see Figure 8.
Freedom	This is a difficult and ambiguous concept to apply in this situation. (See discussion of liberty in D100, Unit 2.)
Co-operation	Probably yes. Voluntary associations are as prevalent as in other areas of urban growth (see Unit 29). But little evidence available on other forms of social interaction.

NB: Most of these assessments are of course simplified summaries of what are often quite complex questions.

Answer SAQ 2 Virtually none. The significance of the suggestion that 'land should be held by society as a whole' is not clear. It is arguable that land is already held by society as a whole as Henry George and others have asserted. The British planning system, for example, gives power to governmental authorities to control changes in the use of all land and property.

Expropriation of rents by the state on the other hand is a more specific proposal. But it would seem likely to be equivalent in its effects to a tax on land and property values. The fact that a particular person pays rent to the state for a piece of property would constitute a recognition of his property rights. This recognition would make it very difficult to prevent the holder of these property rights from entering into some kind of contract with a tenant involving some kind of payment. Payment of rents between individuals and private organizations would thereby continue.

Answer SAQ 3 Howard's interpretation is open to debate. Expropriation of rent would constitute nationalization to the extent that it involved confiscation of assets. But if proper compensation were paid in return for these assets then the question as to whether or not this would constitute nationalization would depend upon whether the acquisition of these assets in fact prevented individuals entering arrangements involving payment for the use of property. If such payments continued, whether or not they were actually called rent, nationalization would arguably have been ineffective.

If payments between individuals for the use of property continued then expropriation of existing rents would, as suggested in the answer to SAQ2, be equivalent to a tax on land and property, which hardly constitutes nationalization.

Answer SAQ 4 A large proportion of the land and property rights in towns developed under the New Towns Acts are held by the development corporations or the New Towns Commission. The development corporations and the New Town Commission are central government bodies akin to the British Railway Board or the BBC so this clearly constitutes nationalization.

The main holders of land and property rights in the expanded towns developed under the 1952 Town Development Act are the receiving local authorities. This form of public ownership would be more generally termed as municipalization.

You might also consider in this context the effects of the 1972 Housing Finance Act. Under the Act power to fix the level of rents for all rented housing accommodation is removed from the hands of local authorities and most private landlords and placed in the hands of the central government. It is arguable that controls of this kind are more akin to nationalization, than say, the kinds of measures advocated by Spencer which were discussed in SAQs 2 and 3, because they considerably reduce the decision making power of individuals, individual landlords and local authorities – including development corporations.

Answer SAQ 5 Physical containment within a defined and limited area.
Self-containment with regard to the provision of facilities such as employment, shops, culture and entertainment, etc. (Ogilvy 1968 suggested that this aim should be re-expressed as 'complete' towns.)

Self-containment with regard to the new town population's activities. The assumption is that the provision of facilities within the town would minimize travel to other areas. The index of commuting independence is a measure of containment in this sense as far as journeys to work are concerned.

Answer SAQ 6   A balance between the levels of employment and population.
A balance in the structure of employment (to give adequate choice of job).
A balance between the level of facilities provided and the size of population.
Social balance. (See Wakefield's ideas quoted by Howard as well as the
discussion in Section 5).
(The first three of the meanings are also covered by the second meaning of the
term self-contained given in the answer to SAQ 5.)

Answer SAQ 7   The index of commuting independence for an area can be defined in the form
of an equation in various alternative terms.
Index of commuting independence

$$= \frac{\text{journeys within an area}}{\text{journeys in} + \text{journeys out}} = \frac{\text{local journeys}}{\text{crossing journeys}}$$

$$= \frac{\text{residents who also work in the area}}{\text{residents working outside area} + \text{persons employed in area living outside}}$$

$$= \frac{\text{internal journeys}}{\text{commuting out} + \text{commuting in}}$$

Answer SAQ 8   Index of commuting independence for central London

$$= \frac{112}{1,192 + 21} = 0.09$$

This is exceptionally low for an area of the size of central London because of the
exceptionally high job ratio. Note that a low index could also be associated with
an exceptionally low job ratio.
Index of commuting independence for Greater London

$$= \frac{3,863}{459 + 111} = 6.8$$

This is exceptionally high because of the size of Greater London in terms of
both employment and population. Note that although the job ratio for Greater
London is near 100 (actually $\frac{3,863 + 459}{3,863 + 111} = 108$) this nevertheless represents
an imbalance between the levels of employment and residents in employment
of nearly 350,000.

Answer SAQ 9   Five. The index of commuting independence in this has its maximum value if
there are no journeys by residents to places outside. So maximum value

$$= \frac{100}{20} = 5$$

Answer SAQ 10   The explanation is that the levels of commuting both to and from the area are
high. This could arise simply because the area for which the index measured
is situated near to other centres of employment and population.

The new town of Cumbernauld fifteen miles from Glasgow is an example of
this kind. The job ratio in 1966 was 96, indicating a close balance between the
levels of employment and population. But the index of commuting independence
was only 0.41. Cumbernauld is one of the exceptions among the new towns in
that first priority in housing has not been given to those with a job in the town.
Instead there have been overspill agreements with Glasgow which give priority
to people in housing need irrespective of where they are employed. Also the
high level of rents in Cumbernauld relative to Glasgow means that many of
those employed in Cumbernauld have been unable to afford the rents in the
new towns (see Thomas 1969b).

Answer SAQ 11   *Managers:*

$$\text{Job ratio} = \frac{1{,}065}{1{,}003} \times 100 = 106$$

$$\text{Index of commuting independence} = \frac{\left(\dfrac{62 \times 1{,}065}{100}\right)}{\left(\dfrac{38 \times 1{,}065}{100}\right) + \left(\dfrac{35 \times 1{,}003}{100}\right)}$$

$$= 0.9$$

Manual workers:

$$\text{Job ratio} = \frac{6{,}570}{6{,}324} \times 100 = 104$$

$$\text{Index of commuting independence} = \frac{\left(\dfrac{79 \times 6{,}570}{100}\right)}{\left(\dfrac{21 \times 6{,}570}{100}\right) + \left(\dfrac{18 \times 6{,}324}{100}\right)}$$

$$= 2.1$$

Note that although there is a close balance between the levels of employment for both managers and manual workers the index of commuting independence is much less for the former than the latter. This is mainly because managers can afford a longer journey to work.

Answer SAQ 12   1 To provide housing at rents which those receiving low incomes can afford.
2 To provide employment which does not necessitate a high level of skills.
London's new towns have been more successful on point 1 than on point 2 though their success even in achieving point 1 is a matter of dispute which was discussed in Section 5.

Scotland's new towns have been more successful on point 2 than point 1. (The average job ratio for unskilled manual workers in Cumbernauld, East Kilbride and Glenrothes in 1966 was 148 – see Thomas 1969b.)

Answer SAQ 13   A sociological charter in this context is a word, phrase, or statement which embodies a particular orientation of values: it projects an idea of the way the world (or part of the world) should be arranged, or makes a claim that this is, despite all arguments to the contrary, the way in which the world *is* arranged.
The concept of a sociological or pragmatic charter derives from Malinowski who argued that the presentation of such a charter is one of the functions of primitive myth (Malinowski 1948).

Answer SAQ 14   The statement assumes that the people living in the area to be affected have sufficient group coherence to warrant description as a 'community' and that, as such, they will respond in a unitary fashion. It may be that there are in fact different sectional groups which will have different reactions, positive or negative, according to their interests. Further, unless opinion is canvassed, it is not possible to say how the residents of the proposed overspill area will react. The council is projecting a view which it would like to be accepted as the view of the residents. At the same time the council is saying how it feels people *ought* to react.

Answer SAQ 15   b, d and e.

Answer SAQ 16   The general level of owner occupation and that of local authority housing has increased at the expense of privately rented dwellings.
In 1947 the earliest year for which data is available only 27 per cent of

dwellings in England and Wales were owner occupied. Only 12 per cent were rented from a local authority or new town development corporation, and 58 per cent were rented from private landlords. By 1966 these percentages were 47, 26, and 23 respectively (see Rollet 1972).

Answer SAQ 17   A reasonable summary would be to say that the principal beneficiaries from the British new towns have been young skilled workers who predominate in their populations. This is the basis for the rather exaggerated charge which is sometimes made that they are 'one-class communities'. You can find evidence on this point in the extract from Heraud's study in Section 5.

The main groups who have not benefited or who have benefited less than Howard, and perhaps later idealists, would have liked can be identified in different ways. As Section 8 of the unit showed, one such group are the tenants of dwellings in new towns. This group of course overlaps considerably with the young skilled workers already labelled as beneficiaries. The level of new town rents has a different impact according to income level of tenants. To tenants of above average income new town rents may be easy to afford. Tenants with relatively high incomes also have the opportunity to transform themselves into owner occupiers with the benefit of a 20 per cent price reduction. But the level of new town rents is high relative to the wages of unskilled workers and high relative to other recipients of below average incomes. New towns provide good housing but not at rents which the poor can easily afford.

The other groups who have not benefited are those with low incomes who are under-represented in the new towns. This includes unskilled workers (as pointed out in Section 5), old age pensioners, and households without any member in employment. Under-representation of these groups has formed the basis for persistent criticism of the new towns.

References   ALONSO, W. (1970) 'What are New Towns For?', *Urban Studies*, 7, 1, pp 37–55.

ASHWORTH, W. (1954) *The Genesis of Modern British Town Planning*, London, Routledge and Kegan Paul.

BEST, R. H. (1972) 'Land Needs in Old and New Towns' in EVANS, HAZEL (ed) (1972) *New Towns: The British Experience*, London, Charles Knight.

BURKE, G. (1971) *Towns in the Making*, London, Edward Arnold.

CHOAY, FRANCOISE (1972) *The Modern City: Planning in the 19th Century*, (translated by HUGO, MARGUERITE and COLLINS, G. R.) London, Studio Vista.

CLAWSON, MARION (1971) *Suburban Land Conversion in the United States: An Economic and Governmental Process*, Baltimore and London, Johns Hopkins Press.

CRESSWELL, P. and THOMAS, R. (1972) 'Employment and Population Balance', in EVANS, HAZEL (ed) (1972) *New Towns: The British Experience*, London, Charles Knight.

EICHLER, E. P. and KAPLAN, M. (1967) *The Community Builders*, University of California Press.

GEE, FRANCES A. (1972) *Homes and Jobs for Londoners in New and Expanded Towns*, Report of a survey carried out by OPCS, London, HMSO.

GOFFMAN, E. (1970) *Strategic Interaction*, Oxford, Blackwell.

HEAP, D. (1963) *An Outline of Planning Law*, London, Sweet and Maxwell.

HERAUD, B. J. (1968) 'Social Class and the New Towns' in *Urban Studies*, 5, 1, pp 33–58.

HOWARD, E. (1898) *Tomorrow: a Peaceful Path to Real Reform*; revised edition (1902) as *Garden Cities of Tomorrow*; paperback edition by Faber and Faber, 1965.

HUTCHINSON, B. (1947) *Willesden and the New Towns*, An Inquiry carried out by the Social Survey for the Ministry of Town and Country Planning, London, Central Office of Information.

MALINOWSKI, B. (1948) 'Myth in Primitive Psychology' in *Magic, Science and Religion and Other Essays*, New York, The Free Press.

MINISTRY OF HEALTH (1935) *Garden Cities and Satellite Towns*, Report of a Departmental Committee, London, HMSO.

MINISTRY OF TOWN AND COUNTRY PLANNING (1946) *First Interim, Second Interim and Final Reports of the Committee on New Towns*, (The Reith Committee), Cmd 6159, 6794 and 6876, London, HMSO.

OGILVY, A. A. (1968) 'The Self-Contained New Town (employment and population)', in *Town Planning Review*, 39, 1, pp 38–54.

OGILVY, A. A. (1971) 'Employment Expansion and the Development of New Town Hinterlands 1961–66', in *Town Planning Review*, 42, 2, pp 113–29.

ORLANS, H. (1952) *Stevenage: A Study of a New Town*, London, Routledge and Kegan Paul.

PAHL, R. E. (ed) (1968) *Readings in Urban Sociology*, Oxford, Pergamon Press (set book).

PETERSON, W. (1969) 'The Ideological Origins of Britain's New Towns', in *American Institute of Planners Journal*.

PURDOM, C. B. (1949) *The Building of Satellite Towns*, London, J. M. Dent & Sons.

REX, J. A. (1968) 'The Sociology of a Zone of Transition' in PAHL, R. E. (ed) (1972).

RICHARDSON, B. W. (1876) *Hygiene, the City of Health*, London, Macmillan.

RODERICK, W. P. (1971) 'The London New Towns: origins of migrants from Greater London up to December 1968 in *Town Planning Review*, 42, 4, pp 423–41.

ROLLET, CONSTANCE (1972) 'Housing' in HALSEY, A. H. (1972) *Trends in British Society Since 1900*, London, Macmillan.

SCHAFFER, F. (1972) *The New Town Story*, Granada Publishing Limited (first published in hardback by McGibbon and Kee, 1970).

THOMAS, RAY (1969a) *London's New Towns – A Study of Self Contained and Balanced Communities*, London, Political and Economic Planning.

THOMAS, RAY (1969b) *Aycliffe to Cumbernauld – A Study of Seven New Towns in their Regions*, London, Political and Economic Planning.

Acknowledgements

Grateful acknowledgement is made to the following sources for material used in this unit:

Text
HMSO for *Report of the New Towns Committee*, Cmd 6876; J. M. Dent & Sons Ltd for C. B. Purdom, *The Building of Satellite Towns*; Faber and Faber Ltd and MIT Press, Cambridge, Massachusetts for Ebenezer Howard, *Garden Cities of Tomorrow*; Political and Economic Planning for R. Thomas, 'London's New Towns – A study of self-containment and balanced communities' in *Political and Economic Planning*, 1969; Longman Group Ltd and the author for Dr B. J. Heraud, 'Social class and the New Towns' in *Urban Studies*, 5, 1, 1968; The Office of Population Censuses and Surveys.

Tables
Table 1: Cambridge University Press for B. R. Mitchell and P. Deane, *Abstract of British Historical Statistics*; *Tables 2 and 3:* Reproduced by permission of the Editor of *Town and Country Planning*. The table appeared in the New Towns Special Issue of January 1973; *Table 4:* Charles Knight and Co. for R. H. Best, 'Provision of land for new and existing towns' in *New Towns: The British Experience*, ed. P. Self. Published by Charles Knight and Co. for the Town and Country Planning Association; *Table 8:* Longman Group Ltd and the author for Dr B. J. Heraud, 'Social class and the New Towns' in *Urban Studies*, 5, 1, 1968; *Table 10:* HMSO for *Reports of the Development Corporations* 1971.

Figures
Figure 1: Mansell Collection; *Figures 3 and 4:* Reprinted by permission of Faber and Faber Ltd and MIT Press, Cambridge, Massachusetts from Ebenezer Howard, *Garden Cities of Tomorrow*; *Figure 9:* New Towns Commission.

The authors of this unit are both members of the New Towns Study Unit in the Open University. Acknowledgement is made to the Social Science Research Council for a grant for a study of *The new town goal of self-containment* which has contributed to some of the ideas expressed in this unit.

Urban development

MILTON KEYNES STRATEGIC PLAN

TOTAL AREA 22,000 ACRES   POPULATION 250,000

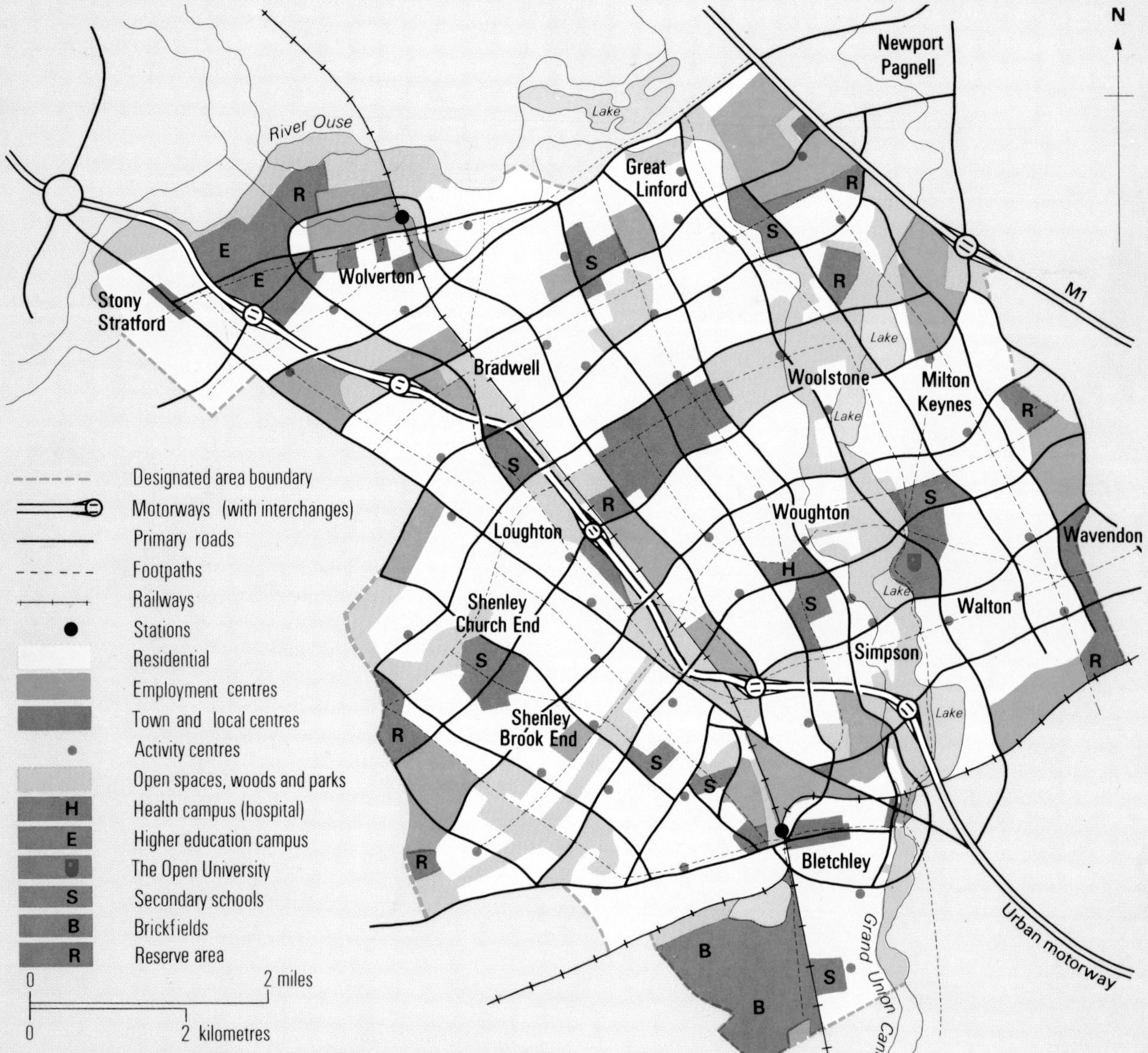
N
Newport Pagnell
River Ouse
Lake
Great Linford
M1
Wolverton
Stony Stratford
Bradwell
Woolstone
Milton Keynes
Loughton
Woughton
Wavendon
Shenley Church End
Walton
Simpson
Shenley Brook End
Bletchley
Grand Union Canal
Urban motorway
Designated area boundary
Motorways (with interchanges)
Primary roads
Footpaths
Railways
Stations
Residential
Employment centres
Town and local centres
Activity centres
Open spaces, woods and parks
H Health campus (hospital)
E Higher education campus
The Open University
S Secondary schools
B Brickfields
R Reserve area
0 2 miles
0 2 kilometres

0 335 01751 7